Valgrind 3.3

Advanced Debugging and Profiling
for GNU/Linux applications

Julian Seward, Nicholas Nethercote, Josef Weidendorfer
and the Valgrind Development Team

Edited and published by Network Theory Ltd.

A catalogue record for this book is available from the British Library.

First printing, March 2008 (5/3/2008).

Published by Network Theory Limited.

15 Royal Park
Bristol
BS8 3AL
United Kingdom

Email: info@network-theory.co.uk

ISBN 0-9546120-5-1

Further information about this book is available from
http://www.network-theory.co.uk/valgrind/manual/

This book has an unconditional guarantee. If you are not fully satisfied with
your purchase for any reason, please contact the publisher at the address above.

The texinfo source files for this manual are available from
http://www.network-theory.co.uk/valgrind/manual/src/

Cover Image: From a layout of a fast, energy-efficient hardware stack.[1] Original
image created with the free Electric VLSI design system by Steven Rubin of Static Free
Software (www.staticfreesoft.com). Static Free Software provides support for Electric
to the electronics design industry.

---

[1] "A Fast and Energy-Efficient Stack" by J. Ebergen, D. Finchelstein, R. Kao, J.
Lexau and R. Hopkins.

Table of Contents

Publisher's Preface

This manual describes the use of Valgrind, a powerful debugging and profiling tool for GNU/Linux programs.

Valgrind is *free software*. The term "free software" has nothing to do with price—it is about freedom. It refers to your freedom to run, copy, distribute, study, change and improve the software. With Valgrind you have all these freedoms.

You can support free software by becoming an associate member of the Free Software Foundation and paying regular membership dues. The Free Software Foundation is a tax-exempt charity dedicated to promoting the right to use, study, copy, modify, and redistribute computer programs. It also helps to spread awareness of the ethical and political issues of freedom in the use of software. For more information visit the website www.fsf.org.

Brian Gough
Publisher
March 2008

1 Introduction

Valgrind is a suite of simulation-based debugging and profiling tools for programs running on Linux (x86, amd64, ppc32 and ppc64). The system consists of a core, which provides a synthetic CPU in software, and a set of tools, each of which performs some kind of debugging, profiling, or similar task. The architecture is modular, so that new tools can be created easily and without disturbing the existing structure.

A number of useful tools are supplied as standard. In summary, these are:

1. Memcheck detects memory-management problems in programs. All reads and writes of memory are checked, and calls to malloc, new, free and delete are intercepted. As a result, Memcheck can detect the following problems:

   - Use of uninitialised memory
   - Reading/writing memory after it has been free'd
   - Reading/writing off the end of malloc'd blocks
   - Reading/writing inappropriate areas on the stack
   - Memory leaks—where pointers to malloc'd blocks are lost forever
   - Mismatched use of malloc/new/new [] vs free/delete/delete []
   - Overlapping src and dst pointers in memcpy() and related functions

   Problems like these can be difficult to find by other means, often remaining undetected for long periods, then causing occasional, difficult-to-diagnose crashes.

2. Cachegrind is a cache profiler. It performs detailed simulation of the I1, D1 and L2 caches in your CPU and so can accurately pinpoint the sources of cache misses in your code. It will show the number of cache misses, memory references and instructions accruing to each line of source code, with per-function, per-module and whole-program summaries. If you ask really nicely it will even show counts for each individual machine instruction.

   On x86 and amd64, Cachegrind auto-detects your machine's cache configuration using the CPUID instruction, and so needs no further configuration info, in most cases.

3. Callgrind is a profiler similar in concept to Cachegrind, but which also tracks caller-callee relationships. By doing so it is able to show how instruction, memory reference and cache miss costs flow between callers and callees. Callgrind collects a large amount of data which is best navigated using Josef Weidendorfer's amazing KCachegrind visualisation tool (http://kcachegrind.sourceforge.net). KCachegrind is a KDE application which presents these profiling results in a graphical and easy-to-understand form.

4. `Massif` is a heap profiler. It measures how much heap memory programs
   use. In particular, it can give you information about heap blocks, heap
   administration overheads, and stack sizes.

   Heap profiling can help you reduce the amount of memory your program
   uses. On modern machines with virtual memory, this reduces the chances
   that your program will run out of memory, and may make it faster by
   reducing the amount of paging needed.

5. `Helgrind` detects synchronisation errors in programs that use the POSIX
   pthreads threading primitives. It detects the following three classes of
   errors:

   • Misuses of the POSIX pthreads API.

   • Potential deadlocks arising from lock ordering problems.

   • Data races—accessing memory without adequate locking.

   Problems like these often result in unreproducible, timing-dependent
   crashes, deadlocks and other misbehaviour, and can be difficult to find
   by other means.

A couple of minor tools (`Lackey` and `Nulgrind`) are also supplied. These
aren't particularly useful—they exist to illustrate how to create simple tools
and to help the valgrind developers in various ways. Nulgrind is the null tool—
it adds no instrumentation. Lackey is a simple example tool which counts
instructions, memory accesses, and the number of integer and floating point
operations your program does.

Valgrind is closely tied to details of the CPU and operating system, and to
a lesser extent, the compiler and basic C libraries. Nonetheless, as of version
3.3.0 it supports several platforms: x86/Linux (mature), amd64/Linux (matur-
ing), ppc32/Linux and ppc64/Linux (less mature but work well). There is also
experimental support for ppc32/AIX5 and ppc64/AIX5 (AIX 5.2 and 5.3 only).
Valgrind uses the standard Unix `./configure`, `make`, `make install` mechanism,
and we have attempted to ensure that it works on machines with Linux kernel
2.4.X or 2.6.X and glibc 2.2.X to 2.7.X.

Valgrind is licensed under the GNU General Public License, version 2.
The `valgrind/*.h` headers that you may wish to include in your code (e.g.
'valgrind.h', 'memcheck.h', 'helgrind.h') are distributed under a BSD-style
license, so you may include them in your code without worrying about license
conflicts. Some of the PThreads test cases, 'pth_*.c', are taken from *Pthreads
Programming* by Bradford Nichols, Dick Buttlar & Jacqueline Proulx Farrell,
ISBN 1-56592-115-1, published by O'Reilly & Associates, Inc.

If you contribute code to Valgrind, please ensure your contributions are
licensed as "GPLv2, or (at your option) any later version." This is so
as to allow the possibility of easily upgrading the license to GPLv3 in future. If you want to modify code in the VEX subdirectory, please also see
VEX/HACKING.README.

1.1 How to navigate this manual

The Valgrind distribution consists of the Valgrind core, upon which are built Valgrind tools. The tools do different kinds of debugging and profiling. This manual is structured similarly.

First, we describe the Valgrind core, how to use it, and the flags it supports. Then, each tool has its own chapter in this manual. You only need to read the documentation for the core and for the tool(s) you actually use, although you may find it helpful to be at least a little bit familiar with what all tools do. If you're new to all this, you probably want to run the Memcheck tool.

Be aware that the core understands some command line flags, and the tools have their own flags which they know about. This means there is no central place describing all the flags that are accepted—you have to read the flags documentation both for Valgrind and for the tool you want to use.

2 Quick Start Guide

This chapter provides a quick start guide for new users of Valgrind.

The Valgrind tool suite provides a number of debugging and profiling tools. The most popular is Memcheck, a memory checking tool which can detect many common memory errors such as:

- Touching memory you shouldn't (e.g. overrunning heap block boundaries, or reading/writing freed memory).
- Using values before they have been initialized.
- Incorrect freeing of memory, such as double-freeing heap blocks.
- Memory leaks.

Memcheck is only one of the tools in the Valgrind suite. Other tools you may find useful are:

- Cachegrind: a profiling tool which produces detailed data on cache (miss) and branch (misprediction) events. Statistics are gathered for the entire program, for each function, and for each line of code, if you need that level of detail.
- Callgrind: a profiling tool that shows cost relationships across function calls, optionally with cache simulation similar to Cachegrind. Information gathered by Callgrind can be viewed either with an included command line tool, or by using the KCachegrind GUI. KCachegrind is not part of the Valgrind suite—it is part of the KDE Desktop Environment.
- Massif: a space profiling tool. It allows you to explore in detail which parts of your program allocate memory.
- Helgrind: a debugging tool for threaded programs. Helgrind looks for various kinds of synchronisation errors in code that uses the POSIX PThreads API.
- In addition, there are a number of "experimental" tools in the codebase. They can be distinguished by the "exp-" prefix on their names. Experimental tools are not subject to the same quality control standards that apply to our production-grade tools (Memcheck, Cachegrind, Callgrind, Massif and Helgrind).

The rest of this chapter discusses only the Memcheck tool. For full documentation on the other tools, and for Memcheck, see the subsequent chapters of this book.

What follows is the minimum information you need to start detecting memory errors in your program with Memcheck. Note that this guide applies to Valgrind version 3.3.0 and later. Some of the information is not applicable for earlier versions.

2.1 Preparing your program

Compile your program with -g to include debugging information so that Memcheck's error messages include exact line numbers. Using -O0 is also a good idea, if you can tolerate the slowdown. With -O1 line numbers in error messages can be inaccurate, although generally speaking Memchecking code compiled at -O1 works fairly well. Use of -O2 and above is not recommended as Memcheck occasionally reports uninitialised-value errors which don't really exist.

2.2 Running your program under Memcheck

If you normally run your program like this:

```
myprog arg1 arg2
```

Use this command line:

```
valgrind --leak-check=yes myprog arg1 arg2
```

Memcheck is the default tool. The --leak-check option turns on the detailed memory leak detector.

Your program will run much slower (e.g. 20 to 30 times) than normal, and use a lot more memory. Memcheck will issue messages about memory errors and leaks that it detects.

2.3 Interpreting Memcheck's output

Here's an example C program with a memory error and a memory leak.

```
#include <stdlib.h>

void f(void)
{
    int* x = malloc(10 * sizeof(int));
    x[10] = 0;          // problem 1: heap block overrun
}  // problem 2: memory leak -- x not freed

int main(void)
{
    f();
    return 0;
}
```

Most error messages look like the following, which describes problem 1, the heap block overrun:

```
==19182== Invalid write of size 4
==19182==    at 0x804838F: f (example.c:6)
==19182==    by 0x80483AB: main (example.c:11)
==19182==  Address 0x1BA45050 is 0 bytes after a block
              of size 40 alloc'd
==19182==    at 0x1B8FF5CD: malloc (vg_replace_malloc.c:130)
==19182==    by 0x8048385: f (example.c:5)
==19182==    by 0x80483AB: main (example.c:11)
```

Things to notice:

- There is a lot of information in each error message; read it carefully.

- The 19182 is the process ID; it's usually unimportant.

- The first line ("Invalid write...") tells you what kind of error it is. Here, the program wrote to some memory it should not have due to a heap block overrun.

- Below the first line is a stack trace telling you where the problem occurred. Stack traces can get quite large, and be confusing, especially if you are using the C++ STL. Reading them from the bottom up can help. If the stack trace is not big enough, use the --num-callers option to make it bigger.

- The code addresses (e.g. 0x804838F) are usually unimportant, but occasionally crucial for tracking down weirder bugs.

- Some error messages have a second component which describes the memory address involved. This one shows that the written memory is just past the end of a block allocated with malloc() on line 5 of example.c.

It's worth fixing errors in the order they are reported, as later errors can be caused by earlier errors. Failing to do this is a common cause of difficulty with Memcheck.

Memory leak messages look like this:

```
==19182== 40 bytes in 1 blocks are definitely lost in
                loss record 1 of 1
==19182==    at 0x1B8FF5CD: malloc (vg_replace_malloc.c:130)
==19182==    by 0x8048385: f (a.c:5)
==19182==    by 0x80483AB: main (a.c:11)
```

The stack trace tells you where the leaked memory was allocated. Memcheck cannot tell you why the memory leaked, unfortunately. (Ignore the 'vg_replace_malloc.c', that's an implementation detail.)

There are several kinds of leaks; the two most important categories are:

- "definitely lost": your program is leaking memory—fix it!

- "probably lost": your program is leaking memory, unless you're doing funny things with pointers (such as moving them to point to the middle of a heap block).

If you don't understand an error message, please consult Section 5.3 [Explanation of error messages from Memcheck], page 45 in the Memcheck chapter which has examples of all the error messages Memcheck produces.

2.4 Caveats

Memcheck is not perfect; it occasionally produces false positives, and there are mechanisms for suppressing these (see Section 3.5 [Suppressing errors], page 15 in the Memcheck chapter). However, it is typically right 99% of the time, so you should be wary of ignoring its error messages. After all, you wouldn't ignore warning messages produced by a compiler, right? The suppression mechanism is also useful if Memcheck is reporting errors in library code that you cannot change. The default suppression set hides a lot of these, but you may come across more.

Memcheck cannot detect every memory error your program has. For example, it can't detect out-of-range reads or writes to arrays that are allocated statically or on the stack. But it should detect many errors that could crash your program (e.g. cause a segmentation fault).

Try to make your program so clean that Memcheck reports no errors. Once you achieve this state, it is much easier to see when changes to the program cause Memcheck to report new errors. Experience from several years of Memcheck use shows that it is possible to make even huge programs run Memcheck-clean. For example, large parts of KDE 3.5.X, and recent versions of OpenOffice.org (2.3.0) are Memcheck-clean, or very close to it.

2.5 More information

Please consult the Valgrind FAQ and the Memcheck chapter, which have much more information. Note that the other tools in the Valgrind distribution can be invoked with the --tool option.

3 Using and understanding the Valgrind core

This chapter describes the Valgrind core services, flags and behaviours. That means it is relevant regardless of what particular tool you are using. The information should be sufficient for you to make effective day-to-day use of Valgrind. Advanced topics related to the Valgrind core are described in the next chapter.

A point of terminology: most references to "Valgrind" in this chapter refer to the Valgrind core services.

3.1 What Valgrind does with your program

Valgrind is designed to be as non-intrusive as possible. It works directly with existing executables. You don't need to recompile, relink, or otherwise modify, the program to be checked.

Simply put `valgrind --tool=tool_name` at the start of the command line normally used to run the program. For example, if want to run the command `ls -l` using the heavyweight memory-checking tool Memcheck, issue the command:

```
valgrind --tool=memcheck ls -l
```

Memcheck is the default, so if you want to use it you can omit the `--tool` flag.

Regardless of which tool is in use, Valgrind takes control of your program before it starts. Debugging information is read from the executable and associated libraries, so that error messages and other outputs can be phrased in terms of source code locations, when appropriate.

Your program is then run on a synthetic CPU provided by the Valgrind core. As new code is executed for the first time, the core hands the code to the selected tool. The tool adds its own instrumentation code to this and hands the result back to the core, which coordinates the continued execution of this instrumented code.

The amount of instrumentation code added varies widely between tools. At one end of the scale, Memcheck adds code to check every memory access and every value computed, making it run 10-50 times slower than natively. At the other end of the spectrum, the ultra-trivial none tool (also referred to as Nulgrind) adds no instrumentation at all and causes in total "only" about a 4 times slowdown.

Valgrind simulates every single instruction your program executes. Because of this, the active tool checks, or profiles, not only the code in your application but also in all supporting dynamically-linked (`.so`-format) libraries, including the GNU C library, the X client libraries, Qt, if you work with KDE, and so on.

If you're using an error-detection tool, Valgrind may detect errors in libraries, for example the GNU C or X11 libraries, which you have to use. You might not be interested in these errors, since you probably have no control over that code. Therefore, Valgrind allows you to selectively suppress errors, by recording them in a suppressions file which is read when Valgrind starts up. The build mechanism attempts to select suppressions which give reasonable behaviour for the C library and X11 client library versions detected on your machine. To make it easier to write suppressions, you can use the `--gen-suppressions=yes` option. This tells Valgrind to print out a suppression for each reported error, which you can then copy into a suppressions file.

Different error-checking tools report different kinds of errors. The suppression mechanism therefore allows you to say which tool or tool(s) each suppression applies to.

3.2 Getting started

First off, consider whether it might be beneficial to recompile your application and supporting libraries with debugging info enabled (the -g flag). Without debugging info, the best Valgrind tools will be able to do is guess which function a particular piece of code belongs to, which makes both error messages and profiling output nearly useless. With -g, you'll get messages which point directly to the relevant source code lines.

Another flag you might like to consider, if you are working with C++, is `-fno-inline`. That makes it easier to see the function-call chain, which can help reduce confusion when navigating around large C++ apps. For example, debugging OpenOffice.org with Memcheck is a bit easier when using this flag. You don't have to do this, but doing so helps Valgrind produce more accurate and less confusing error reports. Chances are you're set up like this already, if you intended to debug your program with GNU gdb, or some other debugger.

If you are planning to use Memcheck: On rare occasions, compiler optimisations (at -O2 and above, and sometimes -O1) have been observed to generate code which fools Memcheck into wrongly reporting uninitialised value errors, or missing uninitialised value errors. We have looked in detail into fixing this, and unfortunately the result is that doing so would give a further significant slowdown in what is already a slow tool. So the best solution is to turn off optimisation altogether. Since this often makes things unmanageably slow, a reasonable compromise is to use -O. This gets you the majority of the benefits of higher optimisation levels whilst keeping relatively small the chances of false positives or false negatives from Memcheck. Also, you should compile your code with -Wall because it can identify some or all of the problems that Valgrind can miss at the higher optimisation levels. (Using -Wall is also a good idea in general.) All other tools (as far as we know) are unaffected by optimisation level.

Valgrind understands both the older "stabs" debugging format, used by gcc versions prior to 3.1, and the newer DWARF2 and DWARF3 formats used by gcc 3.1 and later. We continue to develop our debug-info readers, although the majority of effort will naturally enough go into the newer DWARF2/3 reader.

When you're ready to roll, just run your application as you would normally, but place `valgrind --tool=tool_name` in front of your usual command-line invocation. Note that you should run the real (machine-code) executable here. If your application is started by, for example, a shell or perl script, you'll need to modify it to invoke Valgrind on the real executables. Running such scripts directly under Valgrind will result in you getting error reports pertaining to

/bin/sh, /usr/bin/perl, or whatever interpreter you're using. This may not be what you want and can be confusing. You can force the issue by giving the flag --trace-children=yes, but confusion is still likely.

3.3 The Commentary

Valgrind tools write a commentary, a stream of text, detailing error reports and other significant events. All lines in the commentary have following form:

```
==12345== some-message-from-Valgrind
```

The 12345 is the process ID. This scheme makes it easy to distinguish program output from Valgrind commentary, and also easy to differentiate commentaries from different processes which have become merged together, for whatever reason.

By default, Valgrind tools write only essential messages to the commentary, so as to avoid flooding you with information of secondary importance. If you want more information about what is happening, re-run, passing the -v flag to Valgrind. A second -v gives yet more detail.

You can direct the commentary to three different places:

1. The default: send it to a file descriptor, which is by default 2 (stderr). So, if you give the core no options, it will write commentary to the standard error stream. If you want to send it to some other file descriptor, for example number 9, you can specify --log-fd=9.

   This is the simplest and most common arrangement, but can cause problems when Valgrinding entire trees of processes which expect specific file descriptors, particularly stdin/stdout/stderr, to be available for their own use.

2. A less intrusive option is to write the commentary to a file, which you specify by --log-file=filename. There are special format specifiers that can be used to use a process ID or an environment variable name in the log file name. These are useful/necessary if your program invokes multiple processes (especially for MPI programs). See the basic options section (see Section 3.6.2 [Basic Options], page 18) for more details.

3. The least intrusive option is to send the commentary to a network socket. The socket is specified as an IP address and port number pair, like this: --log-socket=192.168.0.1:12345 if you want to send the output to host IP 192.168.0.1 port 12345 (note: we have no idea if 12345 is a port of pre-existing significance). You can also omit the port number: --log-socket=192.168.0.1, in which case a default port of 1500 is used. This default is defined by the constant VG_CLO_DEFAULT_LOGPORT in the sources.

   Note, unfortunately, that you have to use an IP address here, rather than a hostname.

   Writing to a network socket is pointless if you don't have something listening at the other end. We provide a simple listener program, valgrind-listener, which accepts connections on the specified port and copies whatever it is sent to stdout. Probably someone will tell us this is a horrible security risk. It seems likely that people will write more sophisticated listeners in the fullness of time.

valgrind-listener can accept simultaneous connections from up to 50 Valgrinded processes. In front of each line of output it prints the current number of active connections in round brackets.

valgrind-listener accepts two command-line flags:

- -e or --exit-at-zero: when the number of connected processes falls back to zero, exit. Without this, it will run forever, that is, until you send it Control-C.

- portnumber: changes the port it listens on from the default (1500). The specified port must be in the range 1024 to 65535. The same restriction applies to port numbers specified by a --log-socket to Valgrind itself.

If a Valgrinded process fails to connect to a listener, for whatever reason (the listener isn't running, invalid or unreachable host or port, etc), Valgrind switches back to writing the commentary to stderr. The same goes for any process which loses an established connection to a listener. In other words, killing the listener doesn't kill the processes sending data to it.

Here is an important point about the relationship between the commentary and profiling output from tools. The commentary contains a mix of messages from the Valgrind core and the selected tool. If the tool reports errors, it will report them to the commentary. However, if the tool does profiling, the profile data will be written to a file of some kind, depending on the tool, and independent of what --log-* options are in force. The commentary is intended to be a low-bandwidth, human-readable channel. Profiling data, on the other hand, is usually voluminous and not meaningful without further processing, which is why we have chosen this arrangement.

3.4 Reporting of errors

When an error-checking tool detects something bad happening in the program, an error message is written to the commentary. Here's an example from Memcheck:

```
==25832== Invalid read of size 4
==25832==    at 0x8048724: BandMatrix::ReSize(int, int, int)
                (bogon.cpp:45)
==25832==    by 0x80487AF: main (bogon.cpp:66)
==25832==  Address 0xBFFFF74C is not stack'd, malloc'd
          or free'd
```

This message says that the program did an illegal 4-byte read of address 0xBFFFF74C, which, as far as Memcheck can tell, is not a valid stack address, nor corresponds to any current malloc'd or free'd blocks. The read is happening at line 45 of 'bogon.cpp', called from line 66 of the same file, etc. For errors associated with an identified malloc'd/free'd block, for example reading free'd memory, Valgrind reports not only the location where the error happened, but also where the associated block was malloc'd/free'd.

Valgrind remembers all error reports. When an error is detected, it is compared against old reports, to see if it is a duplicate. If so, the error is noted, but no further commentary is emitted. This avoids you being swamped with bazillions of duplicate error reports.

If you want to know how many times each error occurred, run with the -v option. When execution finishes, all the reports are printed out, along with, and sorted by, their occurrence counts. This makes it easy to see which errors have occurred most frequently.

Errors are reported before the associated operation actually happens. If you're using a tool (e.g. Memcheck) which does address checking, and your program attempts to read from address zero, the tool will emit a message to this effect, and the program will then duly die with a segmentation fault.

In general, you should try and fix errors in the order that they are reported. Not doing so can be confusing. For example, a program which copies uninitialised values to several memory locations, and later uses them, will generate several error messages, when run on Memcheck. The first such error message may well give the most direct clue to the root cause of the problem.

The process of detecting duplicate errors is quite an expensive one and can become a significant performance overhead if your program generates huge quantities of errors. To avoid serious problems, Valgrind will simply stop collecting errors after 1,000 different errors have been seen, or 10,000,000 errors in total have been seen. In this situation you might as well stop your program and fix it, because Valgrind won't tell you anything else useful after this. Note that the 1,000/10,000,000 limits apply after suppressed errors are removed. These limits are defined in 'm_errormgr.c' and can be increased if necessary.

To avoid this cutoff you can use the --error-limit=no flag. Then Valgrind will always show errors, regardless of how many there are. Use this flag carefully, since it may have a bad effect on performance.

3.5 Suppressing errors

The error-checking tools detect numerous problems in the base libraries, such as the GNU C library, and the X11 client libraries, which come pre-installed on your GNU/Linux system. You can't easily fix these, but you don't want to see these errors (and yes, there are many!) So Valgrind reads a list of errors to suppress at startup. A default suppression file is created by the ./configure script when the system is built.

You can modify and add to the suppressions file at your leisure, or, better, write your own. Multiple suppression files are allowed. This is useful if part of your project contains errors you can't or don't want to fix, yet you don't want to continuously be reminded of them.

Note: By far the easiest way to add suppressions is to use the --gen-suppressions=yes flag described in Section 3.6 [Command-line flags for the Valgrind core], page 18.

Each error to be suppressed is described very specifically, to minimise the possibility that a suppression-directive inadvertantly suppresses a bunch of similar errors which you did want to see. The suppression mechanism is designed to allow precise yet flexible specification of errors to suppress.

If you use the -v flag, at the end of execution, Valgrind prints out one line for each used suppression, giving its name and the number of times it got used. Here's the suppressions used by a run of valgrind --tool=memcheck ls -l:

```
--27579-- supp: 1 socketcall.connect(serv_addr)
              /__libc_connect/__nscd_getgrgid_r
--27579-- supp: 1 socketcall.connect(serv_addr)
              /__libc_connect/__nscd_getpwuid_r
--27579-- supp: 6 strrchr/_dl_map_object_from_fd
              /_dl_map_object
```

Multiple suppressions files are allowed. By default, Valgrind uses '$PREFIX/lib/valgrind/default.supp'. You can ask to add suppressions from another file, by specifying --suppressions=/path/to/file.supp.

If you want to understand more about suppressions, look at an existing suppressions file whilst reading the following documentation. The file 'glibc-2.3.supp', in the source distribution, provides some good examples.

Each suppression has the following components:

• First line: its name. This merely gives a handy name to the suppression, by which it is referred to in the summary of used suppressions printed out when a program finishes. It's not important what the name is; any identifying string will do.

• Second line: name of the tool(s) that the suppression is for (if more than one, comma-separated), and the name of the suppression itself, separated by a colon (n.b.: no spaces are allowed), e.g.:

```
tool_name1,tool_name2:suppression_name
```

Recall that Valgrind is a modular system, in which different instrumentation tools can observe your program whilst it is running. Since different tools detect different kinds of errors, it is necessary to say which tool(s) the suppression is meaningful to.

Tools will complain, at startup, if a tool does not understand any suppression directed to it. Tools ignore suppressions which are not directed to them. As a result, it is quite practical to put suppressions for all tools into the same suppression file.

• Next line: a small number of suppression types have extra information after the second line (e.g. the Param suppression for Memcheck)

• Remaining lines: This is the calling context for the error—the chain of function calls that led to it. There can be up to 24 of these lines.

Locations may be either names of shared objects/executables or wildcards matching function names. They begin obj: and fun: respectively. Function and object names to match against may use the wildcard characters * and ?.

> **Important note:** C++ function names must be mangled. If you are writing suppressions by hand, use the `--demangle=no` option to get the mangled names in your error messages.

- Finally, the entire suppression must be between curly braces. Each brace must be the first character on its own line.

A suppression only suppresses an error when the error matches all the details in the suppression. Here's an example:

```
{
  __gconv_transform_ascii_internal/__mbrtowc/mbtowc
  Memcheck:Value4
  fun:__gconv_transform_ascii_internal
  fun:__mbr*toc
  fun:mbtowc
}
```

What it means is: for Memcheck only, suppress a use-of-uninitialised-value error, when the data size is 4, when it occurs in the function `__gconv_transform_ascii_internal`, when that is called from any function of name matching `__mbr*toc`, when that is called from `mbtowc`. It doesn't apply under any other circumstances. The string by which this suppression is identified to the user is `__gconv_transform_ascii_internal/__mbrtowc/mbtowc`.

(See Section 5.4 [Writing suppression files], page 50 for more details on the specifics of Memcheck's suppression kinds.)

Another example, again for the Memcheck tool:

```
{
  libX11.so.6.2/libX11.so.6.2/libXaw.so.7.0
  Memcheck:Value4
  obj:/usr/X11R6/lib/libX11.so.6.2
  obj:/usr/X11R6/lib/libX11.so.6.2
  obj:/usr/X11R6/lib/libXaw.so.7.0
}
```

Suppress any size 4 uninitialised-value error which occurs anywhere in 'libX11.so.6.2', when called from anywhere in the same library, when called from anywhere in 'libXaw.so.7.0'. The inexact specification of locations is regrettable, but is about all you can hope for, given that the X11 libraries shipped on the Linux distro on which this example was made have had their symbol tables removed.

Although the above two examples do not make this clear, you can freely mix `obj:` and `fun:` lines in a suppression.

3.6 Command-line flags for the Valgrind core

As mentioned above, Valgrind's core accepts a common set of flags. The tools also accept tool-specific flags, which are documented separately for each tool.

You invoke Valgrind like this:

```
valgrind [valgrind-options] your-prog [your-prog-options]
```

Valgrind's default settings succeed in giving reasonable behaviour in most cases. We group the available options by rough categories.

3.6.1 Tool-selection option

The single most important option.

- `--tool=<name>` [default=memcheck]

  Run the Valgrind tool called *name*, e.g. Memcheck, Cachegrind, etc.

3.6.2 Basic Options

These options work with all tools.

- `-h --help`

  Show help for all options, both for the core and for the selected tool.

- `--help-debug`

  Same as `--help`, but also lists debugging options which usually are only of use to Valgrind's developers.

- `--version`

  Show the version number of the Valgrind core. Tools can have their own version numbers. There is a scheme in place to ensure that tools only execute when the core version is one they are known to work with. This was done to minimise the chances of strange problems arising from tool-vs-core version incompatibilities.

- `-q --quiet`

  Run silently, and only print error messages. Useful if you are running regression tests or have some other automated test machinery.

- `-v --verbose`

  Be more verbose. Gives extra information on various aspects of your program, such as: the shared objects loaded, the suppressions used, the progress of the instrumentation and execution engines, and warnings about unusual behaviour. Repeating the flag increases the verbosity level.

- `-d`

  Emit information for debugging Valgrind itself. This is usually only of interest to the Valgrind developers. Repeating the flag produces more detailed output. If you want to send us a bug report, a log of the output generated by `-v -v -d -d` will make your report more useful.

- `--tool=<toolname>` [default: memcheck]

  Run the Valgrind tool called `toolname`, e.g. Memcheck, Cachegrind, etc.

- `--trace-children=<yes|no>` [default: no]

  When enabled, Valgrind will trace into sub-processes initiated via the `exec` system call. This can be confusing and isn't usually what you want, so it is disabled by default.

  Note that Valgrind does trace into the child of a `fork` (it would be difficult not to, since `fork` makes an identical copy of a process), so this option is arguably badly named. However, most children of `fork` calls immediately call `exec` anyway.

- `--child-silent-after-fork=<yes|no>` [default: no]

  When enabled, Valgrind will not show any debugging or logging output for the child process resulting from a `fork` call. This can make the output less confusing (although more misleading) when dealing with processes that create children. It is particularly useful in conjunction with `--trace-children=`. Use of this flag is also strongly recommended if you are requesting XML output (`--xml=yes`), since otherwise the XML from child and parent may become mixed up, which usually makes it useless.

- `--track-fds=<yes|no>` [default: no]

  When enabled, Valgrind will print out a list of open file descriptors on exit. Along with each file descriptor is printed a stack backtrace of where the file was opened and any details relating to the file descriptor such as the file name or socket details.

- `--time-stamp=<yes|no>` [default: no]

  When enabled, each message is preceded with an indication of the elapsed wallclock time since startup, expressed as days, hours, minutes, seconds and milliseconds.

- `--log-fd=<number>` [default: 2, stderr]

  Specifies that Valgrind should send all of its messages to the specified file descriptor. The default, 2, is the standard error channel (stderr). Note that this may interfere with the client's own use of stderr, as Valgrind's output will be interleaved with any output that the client sends to stderr.

- `--log-file=<filename>`

  Specifies that Valgrind should send all of its messages to the specified file. If the file name is empty, it causes an abort. There are three special format specifiers that can be used in the file name.

  `%p` is replaced with the current process ID. This is very useful for program that invoke multiple processes. WARNING: If you use `--trace-children=yes` and your program invokes multiple processes and you don't use this specifier (or the `%q` specifier below), the Valgrind output from all those processes will go into one file, possibly jumbled up, and possibly incomplete.

  `%q{FOO}` is replaced with the contents of the environment variable FOO. If the `{FOO}` part is malformed, it causes an abort. This specifier is rarely needed, but very useful in certain circumstances (e.g. when running MPI programs, see Section 5.8 [MPI Wrappers], page 58). The idea is that you specify a variable which will be set differently for each process in the job, for example BPROC_RANK or whatever is applicable in your MPI setup. If the named environment variable is not set, it causes an abort. Note that in some shells, the { and } characters may need to be escaped with a backslash.

%% is replaced with %.

If an % is followed by any other character, it causes an abort.

- `--log-socket=<ip-address:port-number>`

  Specifies that Valgrind should send all of its messages to the specified port at the specified IP address. The port may be omitted, in which case port 1500 is used. If a connection cannot be made to the specified socket, Valgrind falls back to writing output to the standard error (stderr). This option is intended to be used in conjunction with the valgrind-listener program. For further details, see the commentary (see Section 3.3 [The Commentary], page 13) in the manual.

3.6.3 Error-related options

These options are used by all tools that can report errors, e.g. Memcheck, but not Cachegrind.

- `--xml=<yes|no>` [default: no]

  When enabled, output will be in XML format. This is aimed at making life easier for tools that consume Valgrind's output as input, such as GUI front ends. Currently this option only works with Memcheck.

- `--xml-user-comment=<string>`

  Embeds an extra user comment string at the start of the XML output. Only works when `--xml=yes` is specified; ignored otherwise.

- `--demangle=<yes|no>` [default: yes]

  Enable/disable automatic demangling (decoding) of C++ names. Enabled by default. When enabled, Valgrind will attempt to translate encoded C++ names back to something approaching the original. The demangler handles symbols mangled by g++ versions 2.X, 3.X and 4.X.

  An important fact about demangling is that function names mentioned in suppressions files should be in their mangled form. Valgrind does not demangle function names when searching for applicable suppressions, because to do otherwise would make suppressions file contents dependent on the state of Valgrind's demangling machinery, and would also be slow and pointless.

- `--num-callers=<number>` [default: 12]

  By default, Valgrind shows twelve levels of function call names to help you identify program locations. You can change that number with this option. This can help in determining the program's location in deeply-nested call chains. Note that errors are commoned up using only the top four function locations (the place in the current function, and that of its three immediate callers). So this doesn't affect the total number of errors reported.

The maximum value for this is 50. Note that higher settings will make Valgrind run a bit more slowly and take a bit more memory, but can be useful when working with programs with deeply-nested call chains.

- `--error-limit=<yes|no>` [default: yes]

When enabled, Valgrind stops reporting errors after 10,000,000 in total, or 1,000 different ones, have been seen. This is to stop the error tracking machinery from becoming a huge performance overhead in programs with many errors.

- `--error-exitcode=<number>` [default: 0]

Specifies an alternative exit code to return if Valgrind reported any errors in the run. When set to the default value (zero), the return value from Valgrind will always be the return value of the process being simulated. When set to a nonzero value, that value is returned instead, if Valgrind detects any errors. This is useful for using Valgrind as part of an automated test suite, since it makes it easy to detect test cases for which Valgrind has reported errors, just by inspecting return codes.

- `--show-below-main=<yes|no>` [default: no]

By default, stack traces for errors do not show any functions that appear beneath `main()` (or similar functions such as glibc's `__libc_start_main()`, if `main()` is not present in the stack trace); most of the time it's uninteresting C library stuff. If this option is enabled, those entries below `main()` will be shown.

- `--suppressions=<filename>`
  [default: $PREFIX/lib/valgrind/default.supp]

Specifies an extra file from which to read descriptions of errors to suppress. You may use as many extra suppressions files as you like.

- `--gen-suppressions=<yes|no|all>` [default: no]

When set to yes, Valgrind will pause after every error shown and print the line:

```
---- Print suppression ? --- [Return/N/n/Y/y/C/c]
```

The prompt's behaviour is the same as for the `--db-attach` option (see below).

If you choose to, Valgrind will print out a suppression for this error. You can then cut and paste it into a suppression file if you don't want to hear about the error in the future.

When set to all, Valgrind will print a suppression for every reported error, without querying the user.

This option is particularly useful with C++ programs, as it prints out the suppressions with mangled names, as required.

Note that the suppressions printed are as specific as possible. You may want to common up similar ones, e.g. by adding wildcards to function names. Sometimes two different errors are suppressed by the same suppression, in which case Valgrind will output the suppression more than once, but you only need to have one copy in your suppression file (but having more than one won't cause problems). Also, the suppression name is given as <insert a suppression name here>; the name doesn't really matter, it's only used with the -v option which prints out all used suppression records.

- --db-attach=<yes|no> [default: no]

  When enabled, Valgrind will pause after every error shown and print the line:

      ---- Attach to debugger ? --- [Return/N/n/Y/y/C/c]

  Pressing Ret, or N Ret or n Ret, causes Valgrind not to start a debugger for this error.

  Pressing Y Ret or y Ret causes Valgrind to start a debugger for the program at this point. When you have finished with the debugger, quit from it, and the program will continue. Trying to continue from inside the debugger doesn't work.

  C Ret or c Ret causes Valgrind not to start a debugger, and not to ask again.

  Note: --db-attach=yes conflicts with --trace-children=yes. You can't use them together. Valgrind refuses to start up in this situation.

  May 2002: this is a historical relic which could be easily fixed if it gets in your way. Mail us and complain if this is a problem for you.

  Nov 2002: if you're sending output to a logfile or to a network socket, I guess this option doesn't make any sense. Caveat emptor.

- --db-command=<command> [default: gdb -nw %f %p]

  Specify the debugger to use with the --db-attach command. The default debugger is gdb. This option is a template that is expanded by Valgrind at runtime. %f is replaced with the executable's file name and %p is replaced by the process ID of the executable.

  This specifies how Valgrind will invoke the debugger. By default it will use whatever GDB is detected at build time, which is usually /usr/bin/gdb. Using this command, you can specify some alternative command to invoke the debugger you want to use.

  The command string given can include one or instances of the %p and %f expansions. Each instance of %p expands to the PID of the process to be debugged and each instance of %f expands to the path to the executable for the process to be debugged.

  Since <command> is likely to contain spaces, you will need to put this entire flag in quotes to ensure it is correctly handled by the shell.

- `--input-fd=<number>` [default: 0, stdin]

  When using `--db-attach=yes` or `--gen-suppressions=yes`, Valgrind will stop so as to read keyboard input from you when each error occurs. By default it reads from the standard input (stdin), which is problematic for programs which close stdin. This option allows you to specify an alternative file descriptor from which to read input.

- `--max-stackframe=<number>` [default: 2000000]

  The maximum size of a stack frame. If the stack pointer moves by more than this amount then Valgrind will assume that the program is switching to a different stack.

  You may need to use this option if your program has large stack-allocated arrays. Valgrind keeps track of your program's stack pointer. If it changes by more than the threshold amount, Valgrind assumes your program is switching to a different stack, and Memcheck behaves differently than it would for a stack pointer change smaller than the threshold. Usually this heuristic works well. However, if your program allocates large structures on the stack, this heuristic will be fooled, and Memcheck will subsequently report large numbers of invalid stack accesses. This option allows you to change the threshold to a different value.

  You should only consider use of this flag if Valgrind's debug output directs you to do so. In that case it will tell you the new threshold you should specify.

  In general, allocating large structures on the stack is a bad idea, because you can easily run out of stack space, especially on systems with limited memory or which expect to support large numbers of threads each with a small stack, and also because the error checking performed by Memcheck is more effective for heap-allocated data than for stack-allocated data. If you have to use this flag, you may wish to consider rewriting your code to allocate on the heap rather than on the stack.

3.6.4 malloc()-related Options

For tools that use their own version of `malloc()` (e.g. Memcheck and Massif), the following options apply.

- `--alignment=<number>` [default: 8]

  By default Valgrind's `malloc()`, `realloc()`, etc, return 8-byte aligned addresses. This is standard for most processors. However, some programs might assume that `malloc()` et al return 16-byte or more aligned memory. The supplied value must be between 8 and 4096 inclusive, and must be a power of two.

3.6.5 Uncommon Options

These options apply to all tools, as they affect certain obscure workings of the Valgrind core. Most people won't need to use these.

- `--run-libc-freeres=<yes|no>` [default: yes]

  The GNU C library (`libc.so`), which is used by all programs, may allocate memory for its own uses. Usually it doesn't bother to free that memory when the program ends—there would be no point, since the Linux kernel reclaims all process resources when a process exits anyway, so it would just slow things down.

  The glibc authors realised that this behaviour causes leak checkers, such as Valgrind, to falsely report leaks in glibc, when a leak check is done at exit. In order to avoid this, they provided a routine called `__libc_freeres` specifically to make glibc release all memory it has allocated. Memcheck therefore tries to run `__libc_freeres` at exit.

  Unfortunately, in some very old versions of glibc, `__libc_freeres` is sufficiently buggy to cause segmentation faults. This was particularly noticeable on Red Hat 7.1. So this flag is provided in order to inhibit the run of `__libc_freeres`. If your program seems to run fine on Valgrind, but segfaults at exit, you may find that `--run-libc-freeres=no` fixes that, although at the cost of possibly falsely reporting space leaks in 'libc.so'.

- `--sim-hints=hint1,hint2,...`

  Pass miscellaneous hints to Valgrind which slightly modify the simulated behaviour in nonstandard or dangerous ways, possibly to help the simulation of strange features. By default no hints are enabled. Use with caution! Currently known hints are:

  - `lax-ioctls`: Be very lax about ioctl handling; the only assumption is that the size is correct. Doesn't require the full buffer to be initialized when writing. Without this, using some device drivers with a large number of strange ioctl commands becomes very tiresome.

  - `enable-inner`: Enable some special magic needed when the program being run is itself Valgrind.

- `--kernel-variant=variant1,variant2,...`

  Handle system calls and ioctls arising from minor variants of the default kernel for this platform. This is useful for running on hacked kernels or with kernel modules which support nonstandard ioctls, for example. Use with caution. If you don't understand what this option does then you almost certainly don't need it. Currently known variants are:

  - `bproc`: Support the sys_broc system call on x86. This is for running on BProc, which is a minor variant of standard Linux which is sometimes used for building clusters.

- `--show-emwarns=<yes|no>` [default: no]

  When enabled, Valgrind will emit warnings about its CPU emulation in certain cases. These are usually not interesting.

- `--smc-check=<none|stack|all>` [default: stack]

  This option controls Valgrind's detection of self-modifying code. Valgrind can do no detection, detect self-modifying code on the stack, or detect self-modifying code anywhere. Note that the default option will catch the vast majority of cases, as far as we know. Running with `all` will slow Valgrind down greatly. Running with `none` will rarely speed things up, since very little code gets put on the stack for most programs.

  Some architectures (including ppc32 and ppc64) require programs which create code at runtime to flush the instruction cache in between code generation and first use. Valgrind observes and honours such instructions. Hence, on ppc32/Linux and ppc64/Linux, Valgrind always provides complete, transparent support for self-modifying code. It is only on x86/Linux and amd64/Linux that you need to use this flag.

3.6.6 Debugging Valgrind Options

There are also some options for debugging Valgrind itself. You shouldn't need to use them in the normal run of things. If you wish to see the list, use the `--help-debug` option.

3.6.7 Setting default Options

Note that Valgrind also reads options from three places:

1. The file `~/.valgrindrc`

2. The environment variable `$VALGRIND_OPTS`

3. The file `./.valgrindrc`

These are processed in the given order, before the command-line options. Options processed later override those processed earlier; for example, options in `./.valgrindrc` will take precedence over those in `~/.valgrindrc`. The first two are particularly useful for setting the default tool to use.

Any tool-specific options put in `$VALGRIND_OPTS` or the `.valgrindrc` files should be prefixed with the tool name and a colon. For example, if you want Memcheck to always do leak checking, you can put the following entry in `~/.valgrindrc`:

    --memcheck:leak-check=yes

This will be ignored if any tool other than Memcheck is run. Without the `memcheck:` part, this will cause problems if you select other tools that don't understand `--leak-check=yes`.

3.7 Support for Threads

Valgrind supports programs which use POSIX pthreads. Getting this to work was technically challenging but it now works well enough for significant threaded applications to run.

The main thing to point out is that although Valgrind works with the standard Linux threads library (e.g. NPTL or LinuxThreads), it serialises execution so that only one thread is running at a time. This approach avoids the horrible implementation problems of implementing a truly multiprocessor version of Valgrind, but it does mean that threaded apps run only on one CPU, even if you have a multiprocessor machine.

Valgrind schedules your program's threads in a round-robin fashion, with all threads having equal priority. It switches threads every 100,000 basic blocks (on x86, typically around 600,000 instructions), which means you'll get a much finer interleaving of thread executions than when run natively. This in itself may cause your program to behave differently if you have some kind of concurrency, critical race, locking, or similar, bugs. In that case you might consider using Valgrind's Helgrind tool to track them down.

Your program will use the native libpthread, but not all of its facilities will work. In particular, synchronisation of processes via shared-memory segments will not work. This relies on special atomic instruction sequences which Valgrind does not emulate in a way which works between processes. Unfortunately there's no way for Valgrind to warn when this is happening, and such calls will mostly work. Only when there's a race will it fail.

Valgrind also supports direct use of the clone() system call, futex() and so on. clone() is supported where either everything is shared (a thread) or nothing is shared (fork-like); partial sharing will fail. Again, any use of atomic instruction sequences in shared memory between processes will not work reliably.

3.8 Handling of Signals

Valgrind has a fairly complete signal implementation. It should be able to cope with any POSIX-compliant use of signals.

If you're using signals in clever ways (for example, catching SIGSEGV, modifying page state and restarting the instruction), you're probably relying on precise exceptions. In this case, you will need to use --vex-iropt-precise-memory-exns=yes.

If your program dies as a result of a fatal core-dumping signal, Valgrind will generate its own core file (vgcore.NNNNN) containing your program's state. You may use this core file for post-mortem debugging with gdb or similar. (Note: it will not generate a core if your core dump size limit is 0.) At the time of writing the core dumps do not include all the floating point register information.

In the unlikely event that Valgrind itself crashes, the operating system will create a core dump in the usual way.

3.9 Building and Installing Valgrind

We use the standard Unix ./configure, make, make install mechanism, and we have attempted to ensure that it works on machines with kernel 2.4 or 2.6 and glibc 2.2.X to 2.5.X. Once you have completed make install you may then want to run the regression tests with make regtest.

There are five options (in addition to the usual --prefix= which affect how Valgrind is built:

- --enable-inner

  This builds Valgrind with some special magic hacks which make it possible to run it on a standard build of Valgrind (what the developers call "self-hosting"). Ordinarily you should not use this flag as various kinds of safety checks are disabled.

- --enable-tls

  TLS (Thread Local Storage) is a relatively new mechanism which requires compiler, linker and kernel support. Valgrind tries to automatically test if TLS is supported and if so enables this option. Sometimes it cannot test for TLS, so this option allows you to override the automatic test.

- --with-vex=

  Specifies the path to the underlying VEX dynamic-translation library. By default this is taken to be in the VEX directory off the root of the source tree.

- --enable-only64bit

  --enable-only32bit

  On 64-bit platforms (amd64-linux, ppc64-linux), Valgrind is by default built in such a way that both 32-bit and 64-bit executables can be run. Sometimes this cleverness is a problem for a variety of reasons. These two flags allow for single-target builds in this situation. If you issue both, the configure script will complain. Note they are ignored on 32-bit-only platforms (x86-linux, ppc32-linux).

The configure script tests the version of the X server currently indicated by the current $DISPLAY. This is a known bug. The intention was to detect the version of the current X client libraries, so that correct suppressions could be selected for them, but instead the test checks the server version. This is just plain wrong.

If you are building a binary package of Valgrind for distribution, please read README_PACKAGERS. It contains some important information.

Apart from that, there's not much excitement here. Let us know if you have build problems.

3.10 If You Have Problems

Contact us at http://www.valgrind.org/.

See Section 3.11 [Limitations], page 28 for the known limitations of Valgrind, and for a list of programs which are known not to work on it.

All parts of the system make heavy use of assertions and internal self-checks. They are permanently enabled, and we have no plans to disable them. If one of them breaks, please mail us!

If you get an assertion failure in 'm_mallocfree.c', this may have happened because your program wrote off the end of a malloc'd block, or before its beginning. Valgrind hopefully will have emitted a proper message to that effect before dying in this way. This is a known problem which we should fix.

Read the Valgrind FAQ for more advice about common problems, crashes, etc.

3.11 Limitations

The following list of limitations seems long. However, most programs actually work fine.

Valgrind will run Linux ELF binaries, on a kernel 2.4.X or 2.6.X system, on the x86, amd64, ppc32 and ppc64 architectures, subject to the following constraints:

- On x86 and amd64, there is no support for 3DNow! instructions. If the translator encounters these, Valgrind will generate a SIGILL when the instruction is executed. Apart from that, on x86 and amd64, essentially all instructions are supported, up to and including SSE3.

  On ppc32 and ppc64, almost all integer, floating point and Altivec instructions are supported. Specifically: integer and FP insns that are mandatory for PowerPC, the "General-purpose optional" group (fsqrt, fsqrts, stfiwx), the "Graphics optional" group (fre, fres, frsqrte, frsqrtes), and the Altivec (also known as VMX) SIMD instruction set, are supported.

- Atomic instruction sequences are not properly supported, in the sense that their atomicity is not preserved. This will affect any use of synchronization via memory shared between processes. They will appear to work, but fail sporadically.

- If your program does its own memory management, rather than using malloc/new/free/delete, it should still work, but Memcheck's error checking won't be so effective. If you describe your program's memory management scheme using "client requests" (see Section 4.1 [The Client Request mechanism], page 33), Memcheck can do better. Nevertheless, using malloc/new and free/delete is still the best approach.

- Valgrind's signal simulation is not as robust as it could be. Basic POSIX-compliant sigaction and sigprocmask functionality is supplied, but it's conceivable that things could go badly awry if you do weird things with signals. Workaround: don't. Programs that do non-POSIX signal tricks are in any case inherently unportable, so should be avoided if possible.

- Machine instructions, and system calls, have been implemented on demand. So it's possible, although unlikely, that a program will fall over with a message to that effect. If this happens, please report all the details printed out, so we can try and implement the missing feature.

- Memory consumption of your program is majorly increased whilst running under Valgrind. This is due to the large amount of administrative information maintained behind the scenes. Another cause is that Valgrind dynamically translates the original executable. Translated, instrumented code is 12-18 times larger than the original so you can easily end up with 50+ MB of translations when running (e.g.) a web browser.

- Valgrind can handle dynamically-generated code just fine. If you regenerate code over the top of old code (i.e. at the same memory addresses), if the code is on the stack Valgrind will realise the code has changed, and work correctly. This is necessary to handle the trampolines GCC uses to implemented nested functions. If you regenerate code somewhere other than the stack, you will need to use the --smc-check=all flag, and Valgrind will run more slowly than normal.

- As of version 3.0.0, Valgrind has the following limitations in its implementation of x86/AMD64 floating point relative to IEEE754.

  Precision: There is no support for 80 bit arithmetic. Internally, Valgrind represents all such "long double" numbers in 64 bits, and so there may be some differences in results. Whether or not this is critical remains to be seen. Note, the x86/amd64 fldt/fstpt instructions (read/write 80-bit numbers) are correctly simulated, using conversions to/from 64 bits, so that in-memory images of 80-bit numbers look correct if anyone wants to see.

  The impression observed from many FP regression tests is that the accuracy differences aren't significant. Generally speaking, if a program relies on 80-bit precision, there may be difficulties porting it to non x86/amd64 platforms which only support 64-bit FP precision. Even on x86/amd64, the program may get different results depending on whether it is compiled to use SSE2 instructions (64-bits only), or x87 instructions (80-bit). The net effect is to make FP programs behave as if they had been run on a machine with 64-bit IEEE floats, for example PowerPC. On amd64 FP arithmetic is done by default on SSE2, so amd64 looks more like PowerPC than x86 from an FP perspective, and there are far fewer noticeable accuracy differences than with x86.

  Rounding: Valgrind does observe the 4 IEEE-mandated rounding modes (to nearest, to +infinity, to -infinity, to zero) for the following conversions: float to integer, integer to float where there is a possibility of loss of precision, and float-to-float rounding. For all other FP operations, only the IEEE default mode (round to nearest) is supported.

  Numeric exceptions in FP code: IEEE754 defines five types of numeric exception that can happen: invalid operation (sqrt of negative number, etc), division by zero, overflow, underflow, inexact (loss of precision).

For each exception, two courses of action are defined by IEEE754: either (1) a user-defined exception handler may be called, or (2) a default action is defined, which "fixes things up" and allows the computation to proceed without throwing an exception.

Currently Valgrind only supports the default fixup actions. Again, feedback on the importance of exception support would be appreciated.

When Valgrind detects that the program is trying to exceed any of these limitations (setting exception handlers, rounding mode, or precision control), it can print a message giving a traceback of where this has happened, and continue execution. This behaviour used to be the default, but the messages are annoying and so showing them is now disabled by default. Use --show-emwarns=yes to see them.

The above limitations define precisely the IEEE754 'default' behaviour: default fixup on all exceptions, round-to-nearest operations, and 64-bit precision.

- As of version 3.0.0, Valgrind has the following limitations in its implementation of x86/AMD64 SSE2 FP arithmetic, relative to IEEE754.

  Essentially the same: no exceptions, and limited observance of rounding mode. Also, SSE2 has control bits which make it treat denormalised numbers as zero (DAZ) and a related action, flush denormals to zero (FTZ). Both of these cause SSE2 arithmetic to be less accurate than IEEE requires. Valgrind detects, ignores, and can warn about, attempts to enable either mode.

- As of version 3.2.0, Valgrind has the following limitations in its implementation of PPC32 and PPC64 floating point arithmetic, relative to IEEE754.

  Scalar (non-Altivec): Valgrind provides a bit-exact emulation of all floating point instructions, except for fre and fres, which are done more precisely than required by the PowerPC architecture specification. All floating point operations observe the current rounding mode.

  However, fpscr[FPRF] is not set after each operation. That could be done but would give measurable performance overheads, and so far no need for it has been found.

  As on x86/AMD64, IEEE754 exceptions are not supported: all floating point exceptions are handled using the default IEEE fixup actions. Valgrind detects, ignores, and can warn about, attempts to unmask the 5 IEEE FP exception kinds by writing to the floating-point status and control register (fpscr).

  Vector (Altivec, VMX): essentially as with x86/AMD64 SSE/SSE2: no exceptions, and limited observance of rounding mode. For Altivec, FP arithmetic is done in IEEE/Java mode, which is more accurate than the Linux default setting. "More accurate" means that denormals are handled properly, rather than simply being flushed to zero.

Programs which are known not to work are:

- emacs starts up but immediately concludes it is out of memory and aborts. It may be that Memcheck does not provide a good enough emulation of the mallinfo function. Emacs works fine if you build it to use the standard malloc/free routines.

3.12 An Example Run

This is the log for a run of a small program using Memcheck. The program is in fact correct, and the reported error is as the result of a potentially serious code generation bug in GNU g++ (snapshot 20010527).

```
$ valgrind -v ./bogon
==25832== Valgrind 0.10, a memory error detector for x86
==25832== Copyright (C) 2000-2001, and GNU GPL'd, by
                Julian Seward.
==25832== Startup, with flags:
==25832== --suppressions=redhat71.supp
==25832== reading syms from /lib/ld-linux.so.2
==25832== reading syms from /lib/libc.so.6
==25832== reading syms from /lib/libgcc_s.so.0
==25832== reading syms from /lib/libm.so.6
==25832== reading syms from /lib/libstdc++.so.3
==25832== reading syms from valgrind.so
==25832== reading syms from /proc/self/exe
==25832==
==25832== Invalid read of size 4
==25832==    at 0x8048724: BandMatrix::ReSize(int,int,int)
                (bogon.cpp:45)
==25832==    by 0x80487AF: main (bogon.cpp:66)
==25832==    Address 0xBFFFF74C is not stack'd, malloc'd
                or free'd
==25832==
==25832== ERROR SUMMARY: 1 errors from 1 contexts
                (suppressed: 0 from 0)
==25832== malloc/free: in use at exit: 0 bytes in 0 blocks.
==25832== malloc/free: 0 allocs, 0 frees, 0 bytes allocated.
==25832== For a detailed leak analysis, rerun with:
                --leak-check=yes
```

The GCC folks fixed this about a week before gcc-3.0 shipped.

3.13 Warning Messages You Might See

Most of these only appear if you run in verbose mode (enabled by `-v`):

- `More than 100 errors detected. Subsequent errors will still be recorded, but in less detail than before.`

  After 100 different errors have been shown, Valgrind becomes more conservative about collecting them. It then requires only the program counters in the top two stack frames to match when deciding whether or not two errors are really the same one. Prior to this point, the PCs in the top four frames are required to match. This hack has the effect of slowing down the appearance of new errors after the first 100. The 100 constant can be changed by recompiling Valgrind.

- `More than 1000 errors detected. I'm not reporting any more. Final error counts may be inaccurate. Go fix your program!`

  After 1,000 different errors have been detected, Valgrind ignores any more. It seems unlikely that collecting even more different ones would be of practical help to anybody, and it avoids the danger that Valgrind spends more and more of its time comparing new errors against an ever-growing collection. As above, the 1,000 number is a compile-time constant.

- `Warning: client switching stacks?`

  Valgrind spotted such a large change in the stack pointer that it guesses the client is switching to a different stack. At this point it makes a kludgey guess where the base of the new stack is, and sets memory permissions accordingly. You may get many bogus error messages following this, if Valgrind guesses wrong. At the moment "large change" is defined as a change of more that 2,000,000 in the value of the stack pointer register.

- `Warning: client attempted to close Valgrind's logfile fd <number>`

  Valgrind doesn't allow the client to close the logfile, because you'd never see any diagnostic information after that point. If you see this message, you may want to use the `--log-fd=<number>` option to specify a different logfile file-descriptor number.

- `Warning: noted but unhandled ioctl <number>`

  Valgrind observed a call to one of the vast family of `ioctl` system calls, but did not modify its memory status info (because nobody has yet written a suitable wrapper). The call will still have gone through, but you may get spurious errors after this as a result of the non-update of the memory info.

- `Warning: set address range perms: large range <number>`

  Diagnostic message, mostly for benefit of the Valgrind developers, to do with memory permissions.

4 Valgrind core: Advanced Topics

This chapter describes advanced aspects of the Valgrind core services, which are mostly of interest to power users who wish to customise and modify Valgrind's default behaviours in certain useful ways. The subjects covered are:

- The "Client Request" mechanism
- Function Wrapping

4.1 The Client Request mechanism

Valgrind has a trapdoor mechanism via which the client program can pass all manner of requests and queries to Valgrind and the current tool. Internally, this is used extensively to make malloc, free, etc, work, although you don't see that.

For your convenience, a subset of these so-called client requests is provided to allow you to tell Valgrind facts about the behaviour of your program, and also to make queries. In particular, your program can tell Valgrind about changes in memory range permissions that Valgrind would not otherwise know about, and so allows clients to get Valgrind to do arbitrary custom checks.

Clients need to include a header file to make this work. Which header file depends on which client requests you use. Some client requests are handled by the core, and are defined in the header file 'valgrind/valgrind.h'. Tool-specific header files are named after the tool, e.g. 'valgrind/memcheck.h'. All header files can be found in the include/valgrind directory of wherever Valgrind was installed.

The macros in these header files have the magical property that they generate code in-line which Valgrind can spot. However, the code does nothing when not run on Valgrind, so you are not forced to run your program under Valgrind just because you use the macros in this file. Also, you are not required to link your program with any extra supporting libraries.

The code added to your binary has negligible performance impact: on x86, amd64, ppc32 and ppc64, the overhead is 6 simple integer instructions and is probably undetectable except in tight loops. However, if you really wish to compile out the client requests, you can compile with -DNVALGRIND (analogous to -DNDEBUG's effect on assert()).

You are encouraged to copy the 'valgrind/*.h' headers into your project's include directory, so your program doesn't have a compile-time dependency on Valgrind being installed. The Valgrind headers, unlike most of the rest of the code, are under a BSD-style license so you may include them without worrying about license incompatibility.

Here is a brief description of the macros available in 'valgrind.h', which work with more than one tool (see the tool-specific documentation for explanations of the tool-specific macros).

- `RUNNING_ON_VALGRIND`: Returns 1 if running on Valgrind, 0 if running on the real CPU. If you are running Valgrind on itself, returns the number of layers of Valgrind emulation you're running on.

- `VALGRIND_DISCARD_TRANSLATIONS`: Discards translations of code in the specified address range. Useful if you are debugging a JIT compiler or some other dynamic code generation system. After this call, attempts to execute code in the invalidated address range will cause Valgrind to make new translations of that code, which is probably the semantics you want. Note that code invalidations are expensive because finding all the relevant translations quickly is very difficult. So try not to call it often. Note that you can be clever about this: you only need to call it when an area which previously contained code is overwritten with new code. You can choose to write code into fresh memory, and just call this occasionally to discard large chunks of old code all at once.

    Alternatively, for transparent self-modifying-code support, use `--smc-check=all`, or run on ppc32/Linux or ppc64/Linux.

- `VALGRIND_COUNT_ERRORS`: Returns the number of errors found so far by Valgrind. Can be useful in test harness code when combined with the `--log-fd=-1` option; this runs Valgrind silently, but the client program can detect when errors occur. Only useful for tools that report errors, e.g. it's useful for Memcheck, but for Cachegrind it will always return zero because Cachegrind doesn't report errors.

- `VALGRIND_MALLOCLIKE_BLOCK`: If your program manages its own memory instead of using the standard `malloc()` / `new` / `new[]`, tools that track information about heap blocks will not do nearly as good a job. For example, Memcheck won't detect nearly as many errors, and the error messages won't be as informative. To improve this situation, use this macro just after your custom allocator allocates some new memory. See the comments in 'valgrind.h' for information on how to use it.

- `VALGRIND_FREELIKE_BLOCK`: This should be used in conjunction with `VALGRIND_MALLOCLIKE_BLOCK`. Again, see 'memcheck/memcheck.h' for information on how to use it.

- `VALGRIND_CREATE_MEMPOOL`: This is similar to `VALGRIND_MALLOCLIKE_BLOCK`, but is tailored towards code that uses memory pools. See the comments in 'valgrind.h' for information on how to use it.

- `VALGRIND_DESTROY_MEMPOOL`: This should be used in conjunction with `VALGRIND_CREATE_MEMPOOL`. Again, see the comments in 'valgrind.h' for information on how to use it.

- `VALGRIND_MEMPOOL_ALLOC`: This should be used in conjunction with `VALGRIND_CREATE_MEMPOOL`. Again, see the comments in 'valgrind.h' for information on how to use it.

- `VALGRIND_MEMPOOL_FREE`: This should be used in conjunction with `VALGRIND_CREATE_MEMPOOL`. Again, see the comments in 'valgrind.h' for information on how to use it.

- `VALGRIND_NON_SIMD_CALL[0123]`: Executes a function of 0, 1, 2 or 3 args in the client program on the *real* CPU, not the virtual CPU that Valgrind normally runs code on. These are used in various ways internally to Valgrind. They might be useful to client programs.

  Warning: Only use these if you *really* know what you are doing. They aren't entirely reliable, and can cause Valgrind to crash. Generally, your prospects of these working are made higher if the called function does not refer to any global variables, and does not refer to any libc or other functions (printf et al). Any kind of entanglement with libc or dynamic linking is likely to have a bad outcome, for tricky reasons which we've grappled with a lot in the past.

- `VALGRIND_PRINTF(format, ...)`: printf a message to the log file when running under Valgrind. Nothing is output if not running under Valgrind. Returns the number of characters output.

- `VALGRIND_PRINTF_BACKTRACE(format, ...)`: printf a message to the log file along with a stack backtrace when running under Valgrind. Nothing is output if not running under Valgrind. Returns the number of characters output.

- `VALGRIND_STACK_REGISTER(start, end)`: Registers a new stack. Informs Valgrind that the memory range between start and end is a unique stack. Returns a stack identifier that can be used with other `VALGRIND_STACK_*` calls.

  Valgrind will use this information to determine if a change to the stack pointer is an item pushed onto the stack or a change over to a new stack. Use this if you're using a user-level thread package and are noticing spurious errors from Valgrind about uninitialized memory reads.

- `VALGRIND_STACK_DEREGISTER(id)`: Deregisters a previously registered stack. Informs Valgrind that previously registered memory range with stack id `id` is no longer a stack.

- `VALGRIND_STACK_CHANGE(id, start, end)`: Changes a previously registered stack. Informs Valgrind that the previously registered stack with stack id `id` has changed its start and end values. Use this if your user-level thread package implements stack growth.

Note that 'valgrind.h' is included by all the tool-specific header files (such as 'memcheck.h'), so you don't need to include it in your client if you include a tool-specific header.

4.2 Function wrapping

Valgrind versions 3.2.0 and above can do function wrapping on all supported targets. In function wrapping, calls to some specified function are intercepted and rerouted to a different, user-supplied function. This can do whatever it likes, typically examining the arguments, calling onwards to the original, and possibly examining the result. Any number of functions may be wrapped.

Function wrapping is useful for instrumenting an API in some way. For example, wrapping functions in the POSIX pthreads API makes it possible to notify Valgrind of thread status changes, and wrapping functions in the MPI (message-passing) API allows notifying Valgrind of memory status changes associated with message arrival/departure. Such information is usually passed to Valgrind by using client requests in the wrapper functions, although that is not of relevance here.

4.2.1 A Simple Example

Supposing we want to wrap some function

```
int foo ( int x, int y ) { return x + y; }
```

A wrapper is a function of identical type, but with a special name which identifies it as the wrapper for foo. Wrappers need to include supporting macros from valgrind.h. Here is a simple wrapper which prints the arguments and return value:

```
#include <stdio.h>
#include "valgrind.h"
int I_WRAP_SONAME_FNNAME_ZU(NONE,foo)( int x, int y )
{
    int    result;
    OrigFn fn;
    VALGRIND_GET_ORIG_FN(fn);
    printf("foo's wrapper: args %d %d\n", x, y);
    CALL_FN_W_WW(result, fn, x,y);
    printf("foo's wrapper: result %d\n", result);
    return result;
}
```

To become active, the wrapper merely needs to be present in a text section somewhere in the same process' address space as the function it wraps, and for its ELF symbol name to be visible to Valgrind. In practice, this means either compiling to a .o and linking it in, or compiling to a .so and LD_PRELOADing it in. The latter is more convenient in that it doesn't require relinking.

All wrappers have approximately the above form. There are three crucial macros:

I_WRAP_SONAME_FNNAME_ZU: this generates the real name of the wrapper. This is an encoded name which Valgrind notices when reading symbol table information. What it says is: I am the wrapper for any function named foo which is found in an ELF shared object with an empty ("NONE") soname field. The specification mechanism is powerful in that wildcards are allowed for both sonames and function names. The details are discussed below.

VALGRIND_GET_ORIG_FN: once in the the wrapper, the first priority is to get hold of the address of the original (and any other supporting information needed). This is stored in a value of opaque type OrigFn. The information is acquired using VALGRIND_GET_ORIG_FN. It is crucial to make this macro call before calling any other wrapped function in the same thread.

CALL_FN_W_WW: eventually we will want to call the function being wrapped. Calling it directly does not work, since that just gets us back to the wrapper and tends to kill the program in short order by stack overflow. Instead, the result lvalue, OrigFn and arguments are handed to one of a family of macros of the form CALL_FN_*. These cause Valgrind to call the original and avoid recursion back to the wrapper.

4.2.2 Wrapping Specifications

This scheme has the advantage of being self-contained. A library of wrappers can be compiled to object code in the normal way, and does not rely on an external script telling Valgrind which wrappers pertain to which originals.

Each wrapper has a name which, in the most general case says: I am the wrapper for any function whose name matches FNPATT and whose ELF "soname" matches SOPATT. Both FNPATT and SOPATT may contain wildcards (asterisks) and other characters (spaces, dots, @, etc) which are not generally regarded as valid C identifier names.

This flexibility is needed to write robust wrappers for POSIX pthread functions, where typically we are not completely sure of either the function name or the soname, or alternatively we want to wrap a whole set of functions at once.

For example, pthread_create in GNU libpthread is usually a versioned symbol—one whose name ends in, e.g., @GLIBC_2.3. Hence we are not sure what its real name is. We also want to cover any soname of the form libpthread.so*. So the header of the wrapper will be

```
int I_WRAP_SONAME_FNNAME_ZZ(libpthreadZdsoZd0,
                            pthreadZucreateZAZa)
( ... formals ... )
{ ... body ... }
```

In order to write unusual characters as valid C function names, a Z-encoding scheme is used. Names are written literally, except that a capital Z acts as an escape character, with the following encoding:

```
Za      encodes   *
Zp                +
Zc                :
Zd                .
Zu                _
Zh                -
Zs                (space)
ZA                @
ZZ                Z
ZL                (        # only in valgrind 3.3.0 and later
ZR                )        # only in valgrind 3.3.0 and later
```

Hence `libpthreadZdsoZd0` is an encoding of the soname `libpthread.so.0` and `pthreadZucreateZAZa` is an encoding of the function name `pthread_create@*`.

The macro `I_WRAP_SONAME_FNNAME_ZZ` constructs a wrapper name in which both the soname (first component) and function name (second component) are Z-encoded. Encoding the function name can be tiresome and is often unnecessary, so a second macro, `I_WRAP_SONAME_FNNAME_ZU`, can be used instead. The `_ZU` variant is also useful for writing wrappers for C++ functions, in which the function name is usually already mangled using some other convention in which Z plays an important role. Having to encode a second time quickly becomes confusing.

Since the function name field may contain wildcards, it can be anything, including just *. The same is true for the soname. However, some ELF objects—specifically, main executables—do not have sonames. Any object lacking a soname is treated as if its soname was NONE, which is why the original example above had a name `I_WRAP_SONAME_FNNAME_ZU(NONE,foo)`.

Note that the soname of an ELF object is not the same as its file name, although it is often similar. You can find the soname of an object `libfoo.so` using the command `readelf -a libfoo.so | grep soname`.

4.2.3 Wrapping Semantics

The ability for a wrapper to replace an infinite family of functions is powerful but brings complications in situations where ELF objects appear and disappear (are dlopen'd and dlclose'd) on the fly. Valgrind tries to maintain sensible behaviour in such situations.

For example, suppose a process has dlopened (an ELF object with soname) `object1.so`, which contains `function1`. It starts to use `function1` immediately.

After a while it dlopens `wrappers.so`, which contains a wrapper for `function1` in (soname) `object1.so`. All subsequent calls to `function1` are rerouted to the wrapper.

If `wrappers.so` is later dlclose'd, calls to `function1` are naturally routed back to the original.

Alternatively, if `object1.so` is dlclose'd but wrappers.so remains, then the wrapper exported by `wrapper.so` becomes inactive, since there is no way to get to it—there is no original to call any more. However, Valgrind remembers that the wrapper is still present. If `object1.so` is eventually dlopen'd again, the wrapper will become active again.

In short, valgrind inspects all code loading/unloading events to ensure that the set of currently active wrappers remains consistent.

A second possible problem is that of conflicting wrappers. It is easily possible to load two or more wrappers, both of which claim to be wrappers for some third function. In such cases Valgrind will complain about conflicting wrappers when the second one appears, and will honour only the first one.

4.2.4 Debugging

Figuring out what's going on given the dynamic nature of wrapping can be difficult. The `--trace-redir=yes` flag makes this possible by showing the complete state of the redirection subsystem after every mmap/munmap event affecting code (text).

There are two central concepts:

- A "redirection specification" is a binding of a (soname pattern, fnname pattern) pair to a code address. These bindings are created by writing functions with names made with the `I_WRAP_SONAME_FNNAME_{ZZ,_ZU}` macros.

- An "active redirection" is code-address to code-address binding currently in effect.

The state of the wrapping-and-redirection subsystem comprises a set of specifications and a set of active bindings. The specifications are acquired/discarded by watching all mmap/munmap events on code (text) sections. The active binding set is (conceptually) recomputed from the specifications, and all known symbol names, following any change to the specification set.

`--trace-redir=yes` shows the contents of both sets following any such event.

`-v` prints a line of text each time an active specification is used for the first time.

Hence for maximum debugging effectiveness you will need to use both flags.

One final comment. The function-wrapping facility is closely tied to Valgrind's ability to replace (redirect) specified functions, for example to redirect calls to `malloc` to its own implementation. Indeed, a replacement function can be regarded as a wrapper function which does not call the original. However, to make the implementation more robust, the two kinds of interception (wrapping vs replacement) are treated differently.

`--trace-redir=yes` shows specifications and bindings for both replacement and wrapper functions. To differentiate the two, replacement bindings are printed using `R->` whereas wraps are printed using `W->`.

4.2.5 Limitations—control flow

For the most part, the function wrapping implementation is robust. The only important caveat is: in a wrapper, get hold of the `OrigFn` information using `VALGRIND_GET_ORIG_FN` before calling any other wrapped function. Once you have the `OrigFn`, arbitrary calls between, recursion between, and longjumps out of wrappers should work correctly. There is never any interaction between wrapped functions and merely replaced functions (e.g. `malloc`), so you can call `malloc` etc safely from within wrappers.

The above comments are true for {x86,amd64,ppc32}-linux. On ppc64-linux function wrapping is more fragile due to the (arguably poorly designed) ppc64-linux ABI. This mandates the use of a shadow stack which tracks entries/exits of both wrapper and replacement functions. This gives two limitations: firstly, longjumping out of wrappers will rapidly lead to disaster, since the shadow stack will not get correctly cleared. Secondly, since the shadow stack has finite size,

recursion between wrapper/replacement functions is only possible to a limited
depth, beyond which Valgrind has to abort the run. This depth is currently 16
calls.

For all platforms ({x86,amd64,ppc32,ppc64}-linux) all the above comments
apply on a per-thread basis. In other words, wrapping is thread-safe: each
thread must individually observe the above restrictions, but there is no need for
any kind of inter-thread cooperation.

4.2.6 Limitations—original function signatures

As shown in the above example, to call the original you must use a macro
of the form CALL_FN_*. For technical reasons it is impossible to create a single
macro to deal with all argument types and numbers, so a family of macros
covering the most common cases is supplied. In what follows, 'W' denotes a
machine-word-typed value (a pointer or a C long), and 'v' denotes C's void
type. The currently available macros are:

CALL_FN_v_v   Macro
    Call an original function of type void fn (void).

CALL_FN_W_v   Macro
    Call an original function of type long fn (void).

CALL_FN_v_W   Macro
    Call an original function of type void fn (long).

CALL_FN_W_W   Macro
    Call an original function of type long fn (long).

CALL_FN_v_WW   Macro
    Call an original function of type void fn (long, long).

CALL_FN_W_WW   Macro
    Call an original function of type long fn (long, long).

CALL_FN_v_WWW   Macro
    Call an original function of type void fn (long, long, long).

CALL_FN_W_WWW   Macro
    Call an original function of type long fn (long, long, long).

CALL_FN_W_WWWW   Macro
    Call an original function of type long fn (long, long, long, long).

CALL_FN_W_5W   Macro
    Call an original function of type long fn (long, long, long, long, long).

CALL_FN_W_6W   Macro
    Call an original function of type long fn (long, long, long, long, long,
long).

and so on, up to `CALL_FN_W_12W`

The set of supported types can be expanded as needed. It is regrettable that this limitation exists. Function wrapping has proven difficult to implement, with a certain apparently unavoidable level of ickyness. After several implementation attempts, the present arrangement appears to be the least-worst tradeoff. At least it works reliably in the presence of dynamic linking and dynamic code loading/unloading.

You should not attempt to wrap a function of one type signature with a wrapper of a different type signature. Such trickery will surely lead to crashes or strange behaviour. This is not of course a limitation of the function wrapping implementation, merely a reflection of the fact that it gives you sweeping powers to shoot yourself in the foot if you are not careful. Imagine the instant havoc you could wreak by writing a wrapper which matched any function name in any soname—in effect, one which claimed to be a wrapper for all functions in the process.

4.2.7 Examples

In the source tree, `memcheck/tests/wrap[1-8].c` provide a series of examples, ranging from very simple to quite advanced.

`auxprogs/libmpiwrap.c` is an example of wrapping a big, complex API (the MPI-2 interface). This file defines almost 300 different wrappers.

5 Memcheck: a heavyweight memory checker

To use this tool, you may specify `--tool=memcheck` on the Valgrind command line. You don't have to, though, since Memcheck is the default tool.

5.1 Kinds of bugs that Memcheck can find

Memcheck is Valgrind's heavyweight memory checking tool. All reads and writes of memory are checked, and calls to `malloc`, `new`, `free` and `delete` are intercepted. As a result, Memcheck can detect the following problems:

- Use of uninitialised memory
- Reading/writing memory after it has been free'd
- Reading/writing off the end of malloc'd blocks
- Reading/writing inappropriate areas on the stack
- Memory leaks—where pointers to malloc'd blocks are lost forever
- Mismatched use of malloc/new/new [] vs free/delete/delete []
- Overlapping `src` and `dst` pointers in `memcpy()` and related functions

5.2 Command-line flags specific to Memcheck

- `--leak-check=<no|summary|yes|full>` [default: summary]

  When enabled, search for memory leaks when the client program finishes. A memory leak means a malloc'd block, which has not yet been free'd, but to which no pointer can be found. Such a block can never be free'd by the program, since no pointer to it exists. If set to summary, it says how many leaks occurred. If set to full or yes, it gives details of each individual leak.

- `--show-reachable=<yes|no>` [default: no]

  When disabled, the memory leak detector only shows blocks for which it cannot find a pointer to at all, or it can only find a pointer to the middle of. These blocks are prime candidates for memory leaks. When enabled, the leak detector also reports on blocks which it could find a pointer to. Your program could, at least in principle, have freed such blocks before exit. Contrast this to blocks for which no pointer, or only an interior pointer could be found: they are more likely to indicate memory leaks, because you do not actually have a pointer to the start of the block which you can hand to `free`, even if you wanted to.

- `--leak-resolution=<low|med|high>` [default: low]

  When doing leak checking, determines how willing memcheck is to consider different backtraces to be the same. When set to low, only the first two entries need match. When med, four entries have to match. When high, all entries need to match.

For hardcore leak debugging, you probably want to use `--leak-resolution=high` together with `--num-callers=40` or some such large number. Note however that this can give an overwhelming amount of information, which is why the defaults are 4 callers and low-resolution matching.

Note that the `--leak-resolution=` setting does not affect memcheck's ability to find leaks. It only changes how the results are presented.

- `--freelist-vol=<number>` [default: 10000000]

When the client program releases memory using `free` (in C) or delete (C++), that memory is not immediately made available for re-allocation. Instead, it is marked inaccessible and placed in a queue of freed blocks. The purpose is to defer as long as possible the point at which freed-up memory comes back into circulation. This increases the chance that memcheck will be able to detect invalid accesses to blocks for some significant period of time after they have been freed.

This flag specifies the maximum total size, in bytes, of the blocks in the queue. The default value is ten million bytes. Increasing this increases the total amount of memory used by memcheck but may detect invalid uses of freed blocks which would otherwise go undetected.

- `--workaround-gcc296-bugs=<yes|no>` [default: no]

When enabled, assume that reads and writes some small distance below the stack pointer are due to bugs in gcc 2.96, and does not report them. The "small distance" is 256 bytes by default. Note that gcc 2.96 is the default compiler on some ancient Linux distributions (RedHat 7.X) and so you may need to use this flag. Do not use it if you do not have to, as it can cause real errors to be overlooked. A better alternative is to use a more recent gcc/g++ in which this bug is fixed.

You may also need to use this flag when working with gcc/g++ 3.X or 4.X on 32-bit PowerPC Linux. This is because gcc/g++ generates code which occasionally accesses below the stack pointer, particularly for floating-point to/from integer conversions. This is in violation of the 32-bit PowerPC ELF specification, which makes no provision for locations below the stack pointer to be accessible.

- `--partial-loads-ok=<yes|no>` [default: no]

Controls how memcheck handles word-sized, word-aligned loads from addresses for which some bytes are addressable and others are not. When yes, such loads do not produce an address error. Instead, loaded bytes originating from illegal addresses are marked as uninitialised, and those corresponding to legal addresses are handled in the normal way.

When no, loads from partially invalid addresses are treated the same as loads from completely invalid addresses: an illegal-address error is issued, and the resulting bytes are marked as initialised.

Note that code that behaves in this way is in violation of the the ISO C/C++ standards, and should be considered broken. If at all possible, such code should be fixed. This flag should be used only as a last resort.

- `--undef-value-errors=<yes|no>` [default: yes]

  Controls whether memcheck detects dangerous uses of undefined value errors. Set this to no if you don't like seeing undefined value errors; it also has the side effect of speeding memcheck up somewhat.

- `--malloc-fill=<hexnumber>`

  Fills blocks allocated by malloc, new, etc, but not by calloc, with the specified byte. This can be useful when trying to shake out obscure memory corruption problems. The allocated area is still regarded by Memcheck as undefined—this flag only affects its contents.

- `--free-fill=<hexnumber>`

  Fills blocks freed by free, delete, etc, with the specified byte. This can be useful when trying to shake out obscure memory corruption problems. The freed area is still regarded by Memcheck as not valid for access—this flag only affects its contents.

5.3 Explanation of error messages from Memcheck

Despite considerable sophistication under the hood, Memcheck can only really detect two kinds of errors: use of illegal addresses, and use of undefined values. Nevertheless, this is enough to help you discover all sorts of memory-management problems in your code. This section presents a quick summary of what error messages mean. The precise behaviour of the error-checking machinery is described in Section 5.5 [Details of Memcheck's checking machinery], page 51.

5.3.1 Invalid read / Invalid write errors

For example:

```
Invalid read of size 4
   at 0x40F6BBCC: (within /usr/lib/libpng.so.2.1.0.9)
   by 0x40F6B804: (within /usr/lib/libpng.so.2.1.0.9)
   by 0x40B07FF4: read_png_image(QImageIO *)
                  (kernel/qpngio.cpp:326)
   by 0x40AC751B: QImageIO::read()
                  (kernel/qimage.cpp:3621)
 Address 0xBFFFF0E0 is not stack'd, malloc'd or free'd
```

This happens when your program reads or writes memory at a place which Memcheck reckons it shouldn't. In this example, the program did a 4-byte read at address 0xBFFFF0E0, somewhere within the system-supplied library libpng.so.2.1.0.9, which was called from somewhere else in the same library, called from line 326 of 'qpngio.cpp', and so on.

Memcheck tries to establish what the illegal address might relate to, since that's often useful. So, if it points into a block of memory which has already been freed, you'll be informed of this, and also where the block was free'd at. Likewise, if it should turn out to be just off the end of a malloc'd block, a common result of off-by-one-errors in array subscripting, you'll be informed of this fact, and also where the block was malloc'd.

In this example, Memcheck can't identify the address. Actually the address is on the stack, but, for some reason, this is not a valid stack address—it is below the stack pointer and that isn't allowed. In this particular case it's probably caused by gcc generating invalid code, a known bug in some ancient versions of gcc.

Note that Memcheck only tells you that your program is about to access memory at an illegal address. It can't stop the access from happening. So, if your program makes an access which normally would result in a segmentation fault, you program will still suffer the same fate—but you will get a message from Memcheck immediately prior to this. In this particular example, reading junk on the stack is non-fatal, and the program stays alive.

5.3.2 Use of uninitialised values

For example:

```
Conditional jump or move depends on uninitialised value(s)
    at 0x402DFA94: _IO_vfprintf (_itoa.h:49)
    by 0x402E8476: _IO_printf (printf.c:36)
    by 0x8048472: main (tests/manuel1.c:8)
```

An uninitialised-value use error is reported when your program uses a value which hasn't been initialised—in other words, is undefined. Here, the undefined value is used somewhere inside the printf() machinery of the C library. This error was reported when running the following small program:

```
int main()
{
  int x;
  printf ("x = %d\n", x);
}
```

It is important to understand that your program can copy around junk (uninitialised) data as much as it likes. Memcheck observes this and keeps track of the data, but does not complain. A complaint is issued only when your program attempts to make use of uninitialised data. In this example, x is uninitialised. Memcheck observes the value being passed to _IO_printf and thence to _IO_vfprintf, but makes no comment. However, _IO_vfprintf has to examine the value of x so it can turn it into the corresponding ASCII string, and it is at this point that Memcheck complains.

Sources of uninitialised data tend to be:

- Local variables in procedures which have not been initialised, as in the example above.

- The contents of malloc'd blocks, before you write something there. In C++, the new operator is a wrapper round malloc, so if you create an object with new, its fields will be uninitialised until you (or the constructor) fill them in.

5.3.3 Invalid frees

For example:

```
Invalid free()
   at 0x4004FFDF: free (vg_clientmalloc.c:577)
   by 0x80484C7: main (tests/doublefree.c:10)
Address 0x3807F7B4 is 0 bytes
   inside a block of
   size 177 free'd
   at 0x4004FFDF: free (vg_clientmalloc.c:577)
   by 0x80484C7: main (tests/doublefree.c:10)
```

Memcheck keeps track of the blocks allocated by your program with malloc/new, so it can know exactly whether or not the argument to free/delete is legitimate or not. Here, this test program has freed the same block twice. As with the illegal read/write errors, Memcheck attempts to make sense of the address free'd. If, as here, the address is one which has previously been freed, you wil be told that—making duplicate frees of the same block easy to spot.

5.3.4 When a block is freed with an inappropriate deallocation function

In the following example, a block allocated with new[] has wrongly been deallocated with free:

```
Mismatched free() / delete / delete []
   at 0x40043249: free (vg_clientfuncs.c:171)
   by 0x4102BB4E: QGArray::~QGArray(void)
                   (tools/qgarray.cpp:149)
   by 0x4C261C41: PptDoc::~PptDoc(void)
                   (include/qmemarray.h:60)
   by 0x4C261F0E: PptXml::~PptXml(void) (pptxml.cc:44)
Address 0x4BB292A8 is 0 bytes
   inside a block of size 64 alloc'd
   at 0x4004318C: operator new[](unsigned int)
                   (vg_clientfuncs.c:152)
   by 0x4C21BC15: KLaola::readSBStream(int)
                   const (klaola.cc:314)
   by 0x4C21C155: KLaola::stream(KLaola::OLENode
                   const *) (klaola.cc:416)
   by 0x4C21788F: OLEFilter::convert(QCString
                   const &) (olefilter.cc:272)
```

In C++ it's important to deallocate memory in a way compatible with how it was allocated. The deal is:

- If allocated with malloc, calloc, realloc, valloc or memalign, you must deallocate with free.
- If allocated with new[], you must deallocate with delete[].
- If allocated with new, you must deallocate with delete.

The worst thing is that on Linux apparently it doesn't matter if you do mix these up, but the same program may then crash on a different platform, Solaris for example. So it's best to fix it properly. According to the KDE folks "it's amazing how many C++ programmers don't know this".

The reason behind the requirement is as follows. In some C++ implementations, delete[] must be used for objects allocated by new[] because the compiler stores the size of the array and the pointer-to-member to the destructor of the array's content just before the pointer actually returned. This implies a variable-sized overhead in what's returned by new or new[].

5.3.5 Passing system call parameters with inadequate read/write permissions

Memcheck checks all parameters to system calls:

- It checks all the direct parameters themselves.

- Also, if a system call needs to read from a buffer provided by your program, Memcheck checks that the entire buffer is addressable and has valid data, i.e., it is readable.

- Also, if the system call needs to write to a user-supplied buffer, Memcheck checks that the buffer is addressable.

After the system call, Memcheck updates its tracked information to precisely reflect any changes in memory permissions caused by the system call.

Here's an example of two system calls with invalid parameters:

```
#include <stdlib.h>
#include <unistd.h>
int main( void )
{
   char* arr  = malloc(10);
   int*  arr2 = malloc(sizeof(int));
   write( 1 /* stdout */, arr, 10 );
   exit(arr2[0]);
}
```

You get these complaints . . .

```
Syscall param write(buf) points to uninitialised byte(s)
   at 0x25A48723: __write_nocancel (in
                     /lib/tls/libc-2.3.3.so)
   by 0x259AFAD3: __libc_start_main (in
                     /lib/tls/libc-2.3.3.so)
   by 0x8048348: (within a.out)
 Address 0x25AB8028 is 0 bytes
   inside a block of size 10 alloc'd
   at 0x259852B0: malloc (vg_replace_malloc.c:130)
   by 0x80483F1: main (a.c:5)

Syscall param exit(error_code) contains uninitialised byte(s)
   at 0x25A21B44: __GI__exit (in /lib/tls/libc-2.3.3.so)
   by 0x8048426: main (a.c:8)
```

... because the program has (a) tried to write uninitialised junk from the malloc'd block to the standard output, and (b) passed an uninitialised value to exit. Note that the first error refers to the memory pointed to by buf (not buf itself), but the second error refers directly to exit's argument arr2[0].

5.3.6 Overlapping source and destination blocks

The following C library functions copy some data from one memory block to another (or something similar): memcpy(), strcpy(), strncpy(), strcat(), strncat(). The blocks pointed to by their src and dst pointers aren't allowed to overlap. Memcheck checks for this.

For example:

```
==27492== Source and destination overlap in
             memcpy(0xbffff294, 0xbffff280, 21)
==27492==    at 0x40026CDC: memcpy
             (mc_replace_strmem.c:71)
==27492==    by 0x804865A: main (overlap.c:40)
```

You don't want the two blocks to overlap because one of them could get partially overwritten by the copying.

You might think that Memcheck is being overly pedantic reporting this in the case where dst is less than src. For example, the obvious way to implement memcpy() is by copying from the first byte to the last. However, the optimisation guides of some architectures recommend copying from the last byte down to the first. Also, some implementations of memcpy() zero dst before copying, because zeroing the destination's cache line(s) can improve performance.

In addition, for many of these functions, the POSIX standards have wording along the lines "If copying takes place between objects that overlap, the behavior is undefined." Hence overlapping copies violate the standard.

The moral of the story is: if you want to write truly portable code, don't make any assumptions about the language implementation.

5.3.7 Memory leak detection

Memcheck keeps track of all memory blocks issued in response to calls to malloc/calloc/realloc/new. So when the program exits, it knows which blocks have not been freed.

If --leak-check is set appropriately, for each remaining block, Memcheck scans the entire address space of the process, looking for pointers to the block. Each block fits into one of the three following categories.

- Still reachable: A pointer to the start of the block is found. This usually indicates programming sloppiness. Since the block is still pointed at, the programmer could, at least in principle, free it before program exit. Because these are very common and arguably not a problem, Memcheck won't report such blocks unless --show-reachable=yes is specified.

- Possibly lost, or "dubious": A pointer to the interior of the block is found. The pointer might originally have pointed to the start and have been moved along, or it might be entirely unrelated. Memcheck deems such a block as "dubious", because it's unclear whether or not a pointer to it still exists.

- Definitely lost, or "leaked": The worst outcome is that no pointer to the block can be found. The block is classified as "leaked", because the programmer could not possibly have freed it at program exit, since no pointer to it exists. This is likely a symptom of having lost the pointer at some earlier point in the program.

For each block mentioned, Memcheck will also tell you where the block was allocated. It cannot tell you how or why the pointer to a leaked block has been lost; you have to work that out for yourself. In general, you should attempt to ensure your programs do not have any leaked or dubious blocks at exit.

For example:

```
8 bytes in 1 blocks are definitely lost in loss record 1 of 14
    at 0x........: malloc (vg_replace_malloc.c:...)
    by 0x........: mk (leak-tree.c:11)
    by 0x........: main (leak-tree.c:39)

88 (8 direct, 80 indirect) bytes in 1 blocks are definitely lost
                        in loss record 13 of 14
    at 0x........: malloc (vg_replace_malloc.c:...)
    by 0x........: mk (leak-tree.c:11)
    by 0x........: main (leak-tree.c:25)
```

The first message describes a simple case of a single 8 byte block that has been definitely lost. The second case mentions both "direct" and "indirect" leaks. The distinction is that a direct leak is a block which has no pointers to it. An indirect leak is a block which is only pointed to by other leaked blocks. Both kinds of leak are bad.

The precise area of memory in which Memcheck searches for pointers is: all naturally-aligned machine-word-sized words found in memory that Memcheck's records indicate is both accessible and initialised.

5.4 Writing suppression files

The basic suppression format is described in Section 3.5 [Suppressing errors], page 15.

The suppression-type (second) line should have the form:

```
Memcheck:suppression_type
```

The Memcheck suppression types are as follows:

- `Value1`, `Value2`, `Value4`, `Value8`, `Value16`, meaning an uninitialised-value error when using a value of 1, 2, 4, 8 or 16 bytes.

- `Cond` (or its old name, `Value0`), meaning use of an uninitialised CPU condition code.

- `Addr1`, `Addr2`, `Addr4`, `Addr8`, `Addr16`, meaning an invalid address during a memory access of 1, 2, 4, 8 or 16 bytes respectively.
- `Jump`, meaning an jump to an unaddressable location error.
- `Param`, meaning an invalid system call parameter error.
- `Free`, meaning an invalid or mismatching free.
- `Overlap`, meaning a `src` / `dst` overlap in `memcpy()` or a similar function.
- `Leak`, meaning a memory leak.

Param errors have an extra information line at this point, which is the name of the offending system call parameter. No other error kinds have this extra line.

The first line of the calling context: for Value and Addr errors, it is either the name of the function in which the error occurred, or, failing that, the full path of the .so file or executable containing the error location. For Free errors, is the name of the function doing the freeing (e.g., `free`, `__builtin_vec_delete`, etc). For Overlap errors, is the name of the function with the overlapping arguments (e.g. `memcpy()`, `strcpy()`, etc).

Lastly, there's the rest of the calling context.

5.5 Details of Memcheck's checking machinery

Read this section if you want to know, in detail, exactly what and how Memcheck is checking.

5.5.1 Valid-value (V) bits

It is simplest to think of Memcheck implementing a synthetic CPU which is identical to a real CPU, except for one crucial detail. Every bit (literally) of data processed, stored and handled by the real CPU has, in the synthetic CPU, an associated "valid-value" bit, which says whether or not the accompanying bit has a legitimate value. In the discussions which follow, this bit is referred to as the V (valid-value) bit.

Each byte in the system therefore has a 8 V bits which follow it wherever it goes. For example, when the CPU loads a word-size item (4 bytes) from memory, it also loads the corresponding 32 V bits from a bitmap which stores the V bits for the process' entire address space. If the CPU should later write the whole or some part of that value to memory at a different address, the relevant V bits will be stored back in the V-bit bitmap.

In short, each bit in the system has an associated V bit, which follows it around everywhere, even inside the CPU. Yes, all the CPU's registers (integer, floating point, vector and condition registers) have their own V bit vectors.

Copying values around does not cause Memcheck to check for, or report on, errors. However, when a value is used in a way which might conceivably affect the outcome of your program's computation, the associated V bits are immediately checked. If any of these indicate that the value is undefined, an error is reported.

Here's an (admittedly nonsensical) example:

```
int i, j;
int a[10], b[10];
for ( i = 0; i < 10; i++ ) {
  j = a[i];
  b[i] = j;
}
```

Memcheck emits no complaints about this, since it merely copies uninitialised values from a[] into b[], and doesn't use them in a way which could affect the behaviour of the program. However, if the loop is changed to:

```
for ( i = 0; i < 10; i++ ) {
  j += a[i];
}
if ( j == 77 )
  printf("hello there\n");
```

then Memcheck will complain, at the if, that the condition depends on uninitialised values. Note that it doesn't complain at the j += a[i];, since at that point the undefinedness is not "observable". It's only when a decision has to be made as to whether or not to do the printf—an observable action of your program—that Memcheck complains.

Most low level operations, such as adds, cause Memcheck to use the V bits for the operands to calculate the V bits for the result. Even if the result is partially or wholly undefined, it does not complain.

Checks on definedness only occur in three places: when a value is used to generate a memory address, when control flow decision needs to be made, and when a system call is detected, Memcheck checks definedness of parameters as required.

If a check should detect undefinedness, an error message is issued. The resulting value is subsequently regarded as well-defined. To do otherwise would give long chains of error messages. In other words, once Memcheck reports an undefined value error, it tries to avoid reporting further errors derived from that same undefined value.

This sounds overcomplicated. Why not just check all reads from memory, and complain if an undefined value is loaded into a CPU register? Well, that doesn't work well, because perfectly legitimate C programs routinely copy uninitialised values around in memory, and we don't want endless complaints about that. Here's the canonical example. Consider a struct like this:

```
struct S { int x; char c; };
struct S s1, s2;
s1.x = 42;
s1.c = 'z';
s2 = s1;
```

The question to ask is: how large is struct S, in bytes? An int is 4 bytes and a char one byte, so perhaps a struct S occupies 5 bytes? Wrong. All non-toy compilers we know of will round the size of struct S up to a whole number of words, in this case 8 bytes. Not doing this forces compilers to generate truly appalling code for accessing arrays of struct S's on some architectures.

So s1 occupies 8 bytes, yet only 5 of them will be initialised. For the assignment s2 = s1, gcc generates code to copy all 8 bytes wholesale into s2 without regard for their meaning. If Memcheck simply checked values as they came out of memory, it would yelp every time a structure assignment like this happened. So the more complicated behaviour described above is necessary. This allows gcc to copy s1 into s2 any way it likes, and a warning will only be emitted if the uninitialised values are later used.

5.5.2 Valid-address (A) bits

Notice that the previous subsection describes how the validity of values is established and maintained without having to say whether the program does or does not have the right to access any particular memory location. We now consider the latter question.

As described above, every bit in memory or in the CPU has an associated valid-value (V) bit. In addition, all bytes in memory, but not in the CPU, have an associated valid-address (A) bit. This indicates whether or not the program can legitimately read or write that location. It does not give any indication of the validity or the data at that location—that's the job of the V bits—only whether or not the location may be accessed.

Every time your program reads or writes memory, Memcheck checks the A bits associated with the address. If any of them indicate an invalid address, an error is emitted. Note that the reads and writes themselves do not change the A bits, only consult them.

So how do the A bits get set/cleared? Like this:

- When the program starts, all the global data areas are marked as accessible.

- When the program does malloc/new, the A bits for exactly the area allocated, and not a byte more, are marked as accessible. Upon freeing the area the A bits are changed to indicate inaccessibility.

- When the stack pointer register (SP) moves up or down, A bits are set. The rule is that the area from SP up to the base of the stack is marked as accessible, and below SP is inaccessible. (If that sounds illogical, bear in mind that the stack grows down, not up, on almost all Unix systems, including GNU/Linux.) Tracking SP like this has the useful side-effect that the section of stack used by a function for local variables etc is automatically marked accessible on function entry and inaccessible on exit.

- When doing system calls, A bits are changed appropriately. For example, mmap magically makes files appear in the process' address space, so the A bits must be updated if mmap succeeds.

- Optionally, your program can tell Memcheck about such changes explicitly, using the client request mechanism described above.

5.5.3 Putting it all together

Memcheck's checking machinery can be summarised as follows:

- Each byte in memory has 8 associated V (valid-value) bits, saying whether or not the byte has a defined value, and a single A (valid-address) bit, saying whether or not the program currently has the right to read/write that address.

- When memory is read or written, the relevant A bits are consulted. If they indicate an invalid address, Memcheck emits an Invalid read or Invalid write error.

- When memory is read into the CPU's registers, the relevant V bits are fetched from memory and stored in the simulated CPU. They are not consulted.

- When a register is written out to memory, the V bits for that register are written back to memory too.

- When values in CPU registers are used to generate a memory address, or to determine the outcome of a conditional branch, the V bits for those values are checked, and an error emitted if any of them are undefined.

- When values in CPU registers are used for any other purpose, Memcheck computes the V bits for the result, but does not check them.

- Once the V bits for a value in the CPU have been checked, they are then set to indicate validity. This avoids long chains of errors.

- When values are loaded from memory, Memcheck checks the A bits for that location and issues an illegal-address warning if needed. In that case, the V bits loaded are forced to indicate Valid, despite the location being invalid.

  This apparently strange choice reduces the amount of confusing information presented to the user. It avoids the unpleasant phenomenon in which memory is read from a place which is both unaddressable and contains invalid values, and, as a result, you get not only an invalid-address (read/write) error, but also a potentially large set of uninitialised-value errors, one for every time the value is used.

  There is a hazy boundary case to do with multi-byte loads from addresses which are partially valid and partially invalid. See details of the flag --partial-loads-ok for details.

Memcheck intercepts calls to malloc, calloc, realloc, valloc, memalign, free, new, new[], delete and delete[]. The behaviour you get is:

- malloc/new/new[]: the returned memory is marked as addressable but not having valid values. This means you have to write to it before you can read it.

- calloc: returned memory is marked both addressable and valid, since calloc clears the area to zero.

- realloc: if the new size is larger than the old, the new section is addressable but invalid, as with malloc.

- If the new size is smaller, the dropped-off section is marked as unaddressable. You may only pass to realloc a pointer previously issued to you by malloc/calloc/realloc.

- free/delete/delete[]: you may only pass to these functions a pointer previously issued to you by the corresponding allocation function. Otherwise, Memcheck complains. If the pointer is indeed valid, Memcheck marks the entire area it points at as unaddressable, and places the block in the freed-blocks-queue. The aim is to defer as long as possible reallocation of this block. Until that happens, all attempts to access it will elicit an invalid-address error, as you would hope.

5.6 Client Requests

The following client requests are defined in 'memcheck.h'. See 'memcheck.h' for exact details of their arguments.

- VALGRIND_MAKE_MEM_NOACCESS, VALGRIND_MAKE_MEM_UNDEFINED and VALGRIND_MAKE_MEM_DEFINED. These mark address ranges as completely inaccessible, accessible but containing undefined data, and accessible and containing defined data, respectively. Subsequent errors may have their faulting addresses described in terms of these blocks. Returns a "block handle". Returns zero when not run on Valgrind.

- VALGRIND_MAKE_MEM_DEFINED_IF_ADDRESSABLE. This is just like VALGRIND_MAKE_MEM_DEFINED but only affects those bytes that are already addressable.

- VALGRIND_DISCARD: At some point you may want Valgrind to stop reporting errors in terms of the blocks defined by the previous three macros. To do this, the above macros return a small-integer "block handle". You can pass this block handle to VALGRIND_DISCARD. After doing so, Valgrind will no longer be able to relate addressing errors to the user-defined block associated with the handle. The permissions settings associated with the handle remain in place; this just affects how errors are reported, not whether they are reported. Returns 1 for an invalid handle and 0 for a valid handle (although passing invalid handles is harmless). Always returns 0 when not run on Valgrind.

- VALGRIND_CHECK_MEM_IS_ADDRESSABLE and VALGRIND_CHECK_MEM_IS_DEFINED: check immediately whether or not the given address range has the relevant property, and if not, print an error message. Also, for the convenience of the client, returns zero if the relevant property holds; otherwise, the returned value is the address of the first byte for which the property is not true. Always returns 0 when not run on Valgrind.

- VALGRIND_CHECK_VALUE_IS_DEFINED: a quick and easy way to find out whether Valgrind thinks a particular value (lvalue, to be precise) is addressable and defined. Prints an error message if not. Returns no value.

- VALGRIND_DO_LEAK_CHECK: runs the memory leak detector right now. Is useful for incrementally checking for leaks between arbitrary places in the program's execution. Returns no value.

- VALGRIND_COUNT_LEAKS: fills in the four arguments with the number of bytes of memory found by the previous leak check to be leaked, dubious, reachable and suppressed. Again, useful in test harness code, after calling VALGRIND_DO_LEAK_CHECK.

- VALGRIND_GET_VBITS and VALGRIND_SET_VBITS: allow you to get and set the V (validity) bits for an address range. You should probably only set V bits that you have got with VALGRIND_GET_VBITS. Only for those who really know what they are doing.

5.7 Memory Pools: describing and working with custom allocators

Some programs use custom memory allocators, often for performance reasons. Left to itself, Memcheck is unable to "understand" the behaviour of custom allocation schemes and so may miss errors and leaks in your program. What this section describes is a way to give Memcheck enough of a description of your custom allocator that it can make at least some sense of what is happening.

There are many different sorts of custom allocator, so Memcheck attempts to reason about them using a loose, abstract model. We use the following terminology when describing custom allocation systems:

- Custom allocation involves a set of independent "memory pools".

- Memcheck's notion of a a memory pool consists of a single "anchor address" and a set of non-overlapping "chunks" associated with the anchor address.

- Typically a pool's anchor address is the address of a book-keeping "header" structure.

- Typically the pool's chunks are drawn from a contiguous "superblock" acquired through the system malloc() or mmap().

Keep in mind that the last two points above say "typically": the Valgrind mempool client request API is intentionally vague about the exact structure of a mempool. There is no specific mention made of headers or superblocks. Nevertheless, the following picture may help elucidate the intention of the terms in the API:

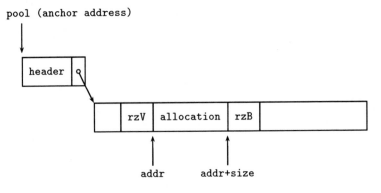

Note that the header and the superblock may be contiguous or discontiguous, and there may be multiple superblocks associated with a single header; such variations are opaque to Memcheck. The API only requires that your allocation scheme can present sensible values of "pool", "addr" and "size".

Typically, before making client requests related to mempools, a client program will have allocated such a header and superblock for their mempool, and marked the superblock NOACCESS using the VALGRIND_MAKE_MEM_NOACCESS client request.

When dealing with mempools, the goal is to maintain a particular invariant condition: that Memcheck believes the unallocated portions of the pool's superblock (including redzones) are NOACCESS. To maintain this invariant, the client program must ensure that the superblock starts out in that state; Memcheck cannot make it so, since Memcheck never explicitly learns about the superblock of a pool, only the allocated chunks within the pool.

Once the header and superblock for a pool are established and properly marked, there are a number of client requests programs can use to inform Memcheck about changes to the state of a mempool:

- VALGRIND_CREATE_MEMPOOL(pool, rzB, is_zeroed): This request registers the address pool as the anchor address for a memory pool. It also provides a size rzB, specifying how large the redzones placed around chunks allocated from the pool should be. Finally, it provides an is_zeroed flag that specifies whether the pool's chunks are zeroed (more precisely: defined) when allocated.

  Upon completion of this request, no chunks are associated with the pool. The request simply tells Memcheck that the pool exists, so that subsequent calls can refer to it as a pool.

- VALGRIND_DESTROY_MEMPOOL(pool): This request tells Memcheck that a pool is being torn down. Memcheck then removes all records of chunks associated with the pool, as well as its record of the pool's existence. While destroying its records of a mempool, Memcheck resets the redzones of any live chunks in the pool to NOACCESS.

- VALGRIND_MEMPOOL_ALLOC(pool, addr, size): This request informs Memcheck that a size-byte chunk has been allocated at addr, and associates the chunk with the specified pool. If the pool was created with nonzero rzB redzones, Memcheck will mark the rzB bytes before and after the chunk as NOACCESS. If the pool was created with the is_zeroed flag set, Memcheck will mark the chunk as DEFINED, otherwise Memcheck will mark the chunk as UNDEFINED.

- VALGRIND_MEMPOOL_FREE(pool, addr): This request informs Memcheck that the chunk at addr should no longer be considered allocated. Memcheck will mark the chunk associated with addr as NOACCESS, and delete its record of the chunk's existence.

- VALGRIND_MEMPOOL_TRIM(pool, addr, size): This request "trims" the chunks associated with pool. The request only operates on chunks associated with pool. Trimming is formally defined as:

  - All chunks entirely inside the range [addr,addr+size) are preserved.

- All chunks entirely outside the range [addr,addr+size) are discarded, as though VALGRIND_MEMPOOL_FREE was called on them.
- All other chunks must intersect with the range [addr,addr+size); areas outside the intersection are marked as NOACCESS, as though they had been independently freed with VALGRIND_MEMPOOL_FREE.

  This is a somewhat rare request, but can be useful in implementing the type of mass-free operations common in custom LIFO allocators.
- VALGRIND_MOVE_MEMPOOL(poolA, poolB): This request informs Memcheck that the pool previously anchored at address poolA has moved to anchor address poolB. This is a rare request, typically only needed if you realloc() the header of a mempool.

  No memory-status bits are altered by this request.
- VALGRIND_MEMPOOL_CHANGE(pool, addrA, addrB, size): This request informs Memcheck that the chunk previously allocated at address addrA within pool has been moved and/or resized, and should be changed to cover the region [addrB,addrB+size). This is a rare request, typically only needed if you realloc() a superblock or wish to extend a chunk without changing its memory-status bits.

  No memory-status bits are altered by this request.
- VALGRIND_MEMPOOL_EXISTS(pool):   This request informs the caller whether or not Memcheck is currently tracking a mempool at anchor address pool. It evaluates to 1 when there is a mempool associated with that address, 0 otherwise. This is a rare request, only useful in circumstances when client code might have lost track of the set of active mempools.

5.8 Debugging MPI Parallel Programs with Valgrind

Valgrind supports debugging of distributed-memory applications which use the MPI message passing standard. This support consists of a library of wrapper functions for the PMPI_* interface. When incorporated into the application's address space, either by direct linking or by LD_PRELOAD, the wrappers intercept calls to PMPI_Send, PMPI_Recv, etc. They then use client requests to inform Valgrind of memory state changes caused by the function being wrapped. This reduces the number of false positives that Memcheck otherwise typically reports for MPI applications.

The wrappers also take the opportunity to carefully check size and definedness of buffers passed as arguments to MPI functions, hence detecting errors such as passing undefined data to PMPI_Send, or receiving data into a buffer which is too small.

Unlike most of the rest of Valgrind, the wrapper library is subject to a BSD-style license, so you can link it into any code base you like. See the top of auxprogs/libmpiwrap.c for license details.

5.8.1 Building and installing the MPI wrappers

The wrapper library will be built automatically if possible. Valgrind's configure script will look for a suitable mpicc to build it with. This must be the same mpicc you use to build the MPI application you want to debug. By default, Valgrind tries mpicc, but you can specify a different one by using the configure-time flag --with-mpicc=. Currently the wrappers are only buildable with mpiccs which are based on GNU gcc or Intel's icc.

Check that the configure script prints a line like this:

```
checking for MPI2-compliant mpicc and mpi.h... yes, mpicc
```

If it says ... no, your mpicc has failed to compile and link a test MPI2 program.

If the configure test succeeds, continue in the usual way with make and make install. The final install tree should then contain libmpiwrap.so.

Compile up a test MPI program (e.g., MPI hello-world) and try this:

```
LD_PRELOAD=$prefix/lib/valgrind/<platform>/libmpiwrap.so \
        mpirun [args] $prefix/bin/valgrind ./hello
```

You should see something similar to the following

```
valgrind MPI wrappers 31901: Active for pid 31901
valgrind MPI wrappers 31901: Try MPIWRAP_DEBUG=help for
  possible options
```

repeated for every process in the group. If you do not see these, there is an build/installation problem of some kind.

The MPI functions to be wrapped are assumed to be in an ELF shared object with soname matching libmpi.so*. This is known to be correct at least for Open MPI and Quadrics MPI, and can easily be changed if required.

5.8.2 Getting started

Compile your MPI application as usual, taking care to link it using the same mpicc that your Valgrind build was configured with.

Use the following basic scheme to run your application on Valgrind with the wrappers engaged:

```
MPIWRAP_DEBUG=[wrapper-args] \
LD_PRELOAD=$prefix/lib/valgrind/<platform>/libmpiwrap.so \
    mpirun [mpirun-args] \
    $prefix/bin/valgrind [valgrind-args] \
    [application] [app-args]
```

As an alternative to LD_PRELOADing libmpiwrap.so, you can simply link it to your application if desired. This should not disturb native behaviour of your application in any way.

5.8.3 Controlling the MPI wrapper library

Environment variable `MPIWRAP_DEBUG` is consulted at startup. The default behaviour is to print a starting banner

```
valgrind MPI wrappers 16386: Active for pid 16386
valgrind MPI wrappers 16386: Try MPIWRAP_DEBUG=help for
  possible options
```

and then be relatively quiet.

You can give a list of comma-separated options in `MPIWRAP_DEBUG`. These are

- `verbose`: show entries/exits of all wrappers. Also show extra debugging info, such as the status of outstanding `MPI_Requests` resulting from uncompleted `MPI_Irecvs`.

- `quiet`: opposite of `verbose`, only print anything when the wrappers want to report a detected programming error, or in case of catastrophic failure of the wrappers.

- `warn`: by default, functions which lack proper wrappers are not commented on, just silently ignored. This causes a warning to be printed for each unwrapped function used, up to a maximum of three warnings per function.

- `strict`: print an error message and abort the program if a function lacking a wrapper is used.

If you want to use Valgrind's XML output facility (`--xml=yes`), you should pass `quiet` in `MPIWRAP_DEBUG` so as to get rid of any extraneous printing from the wrappers.

5.8.4 Abilities and limitations

5.8.4.1 Functions

All MPI2 functions except `MPI_Wtick`, `MPI_Wtime` and `MPI_Pcontrol` have wrappers. The first two are not wrapped because they return a double, and Valgrind's function-wrap mechanism cannot handle that (it could easily enough be extended to). `MPI_Pcontrol` cannot be wrapped as it has variable arity: int `MPI_Pcontrol(const int level, ...)`

Most functions are wrapped with a default wrapper which does nothing except complain or abort if it is called, depending on settings in `MPIWRAP_DEBUG` listed above. The following functions have "real", do-something-useful wrappers:

```
PMPI_Send PMPI_Bsend PMPI_Ssend PMPI_Rsend
PMPI_Recv PMPI_Get_count
PMPI_Isend PMPI_Ibsend PMPI_Issend PMPI_Irsend

PMPI_Irecv
PMPI_Wait PMPI_Waitall
PMPI_Test PMPI_Testall

PMPI_Iprobe PMPI_Probe

PMPI_Cancel
```

```
PMPI_Sendrecv

PMPI_Type_commit PMPI_Type_free

PMPI_Pack PMPI_Unpack

PMPI_Bcast PMPI_Gather PMPI_Scatter PMPI_Alltoall
PMPI_Reduce PMPI_Allreduce PMPI_Op_create

PMPI_Comm_create PMPI_Comm_dup PMPI_Comm_free
PMPI_Comm_rank PMPI_Comm_size

PMPI_Error_string
PMPI_Init PMPI_Initialized PMPI_Finalize
```

A few functions such as PMPI_Address are listed as HAS_NO_WRAPPER. They have no wrapper at all as there is nothing worth checking, and giving a no-op wrapper would reduce performance for no reason.

Note that the wrapper library itself can itself generate large numbers of calls to the MPI implementation, especially when walking complex types. The most common functions called are PMPI_Extent, PMPI_Type_get_envelope, PMPI_Type_get_contents, and PMPI_Type_free.

5.8.4.2 Types

MPI-1.1 structured types are supported, and walked exactly. The currently supported combiners are MPI_COMBINER_NAMED, MPI_COMBINER_CONTIGUOUS, MPI_COMBINER_VECTOR, MPI_COMBINER_HVECTOR MPI_COMBINER_INDEXED, MPI_COMBINER_HINDEXED and MPI_COMBINER_STRUCT. This should cover all MPI-1.1 types. The mechanism (function walk_type) should extend easily to cover MPI2 combiners.

MPI defines some named structured types (MPI_FLOAT_INT, MPI_DOUBLE_INT, MPI_LONG_INT, MPI_2INT, MPI_SHORT_INT, MPI_LONG_DOUBLE_INT) which are pairs of some basic type and a C int. Unfortunately the MPI specification makes it impossible to look inside these types and see where the fields are. Therefore these wrappers assume the types are laid out as struct { float val; int loc; } (for MPI_FLOAT_INT), etc, and act accordingly. This appears to be correct at least for Open MPI 1.0.2 and for Quadrics MPI.

If strict is an option specified in MPIWRAP_DEBUG, the application will abort if an unhandled type is encountered. Otherwise, the application will print a warning message and continue.

Some effort is made to mark/check memory ranges corresponding to arrays of values in a single pass. This is important for performance since asking Valgrind to mark/check any range, no matter how small, carries quite a large constant cost. This optimisation is applied to arrays of primitive types (double, float, int, long, long long, short, char, and long double on platforms where sizeof(long double) == 8). For arrays of all other types, the wrappers handle each element individually and so there can be a very large performance cost.

5.8.5 Writing new MPI function wrappers

For the most part the wrappers are straightforward. The only significant complexity arises with nonblocking receives.

The issue is that MPI_Irecv states the recv buffer and returns immediately, giving a handle (MPI_Request) for the transaction. Later the user will have to poll for completion with MPI_Wait etc, and when the transaction completes successfully, the wrappers have to paint the recv buffer. But the recv buffer details are not presented to MPI_Wait—only the handle is. The library therefore maintains a shadow table which associates uncompleted MPI_Requests with the corresponding buffer address/count/type. When an operation completes, the table is searched for the associated address/count/type info, and memory is marked accordingly.

Access to the table is guarded by a (POSIX pthreads) lock, so as to make the library thread-safe.

The table is allocated with malloc and never freed, so it will show up in leak checks.

Writing new wrappers should be fairly easy. The source file is auxprogs/libmpiwrap.c. If possible, find an existing wrapper for a function of similar behaviour to the one you want to wrap, and use it as a starting point. The wrappers are organised in sections in the same order as the MPI 1.1 spec, to aid navigation. When adding a wrapper, remember to comment out the definition of the default wrapper in the long list of defaults at the bottom of the file (do not remove it, just comment it out).

5.8.6 What to expect when using the MPI wrappers

The wrappers should reduce Memcheck's false-error rate on MPI applications. Because the wrapping is done at the MPI interface, there will still potentially be a large number of errors reported in the MPI implementation below the interface. The best you can do is try to suppress them.

You may also find that the input-side (buffer length/definedness) checks find errors in your MPI use, for example passing too short a buffer to MPI_Recv.

Functions which are not wrapped may increase the false error rate. A possible approach is to run with MPI_DEBUG containing warn. This will show you functions which lack proper wrappers but which are nevertheless used. You can then write wrappers for them.

A known source of potential false errors are the PMPI_Reduce family of functions, when using a custom (user-defined) reduction function. In a reduction operation, each node notionally sends data to a "central point" which uses the specified reduction function to merge the data items into a single item. Hence, in general, data is passed between nodes and fed to the reduction function, but the wrapper library cannot mark the transferred data as initialised before it is handed to the reduction function, because all that happens "inside" the PMPI_Reduce call. As a result you may see false positives reported in your reduction function.

6 Cachegrind: a cache and branch profiler

6.1 Cache and branch profiling

To use this tool, you must specify --tool=cachegrind on the Valgrind command line.

Cachegrind is a tool for finding places where programs interact badly with typical modern superscalar processors and run slowly as a result. In particular, it will do a cache simulation of your program, and optionally a branch-predictor simulation, and can then annotate your source line-by-line with the number of cache misses and branch mispredictions. The following statistics are collected:

- L1 instruction cache reads and misses;
- L1 data cache reads and read misses, writes and write misses;
- L2 unified cache reads and read misses, writes and writes misses.
- Conditional branches and mispredicted conditional branches.
- Indirect branches and mispredicted indirect branches. An indirect branch is a jump or call to a destination only known at run time.

On a modern machine, an L1 miss will typically cost around 10 cycles, an L2 miss can cost as much as 200 cycles, and a mispredicted branch costs in the region of 10 to 30 cycles. Detailed cache and branch profiling can be very useful for improving the performance of your program.

Also, since one instruction cache read is performed per instruction executed, you can find out how many instructions are executed per line, which can be useful for traditional profiling and test coverage.

Branch profiling is not enabled by default. To use it, you must additionally specify --branch-sim=yes on the command line.

6.1.1 Overview

First off, as for normal Valgrind use, you probably want to compile with debugging info (the -g flag). But by contrast with normal Valgrind use, you probably do want to turn optimisation on, since you should profile your program as it will be normally run.

The two steps are:

1. Run your program with valgrind --tool=cachegrind in front of the normal command line invocation. When the program finishes, Cachegrind will print summary cache statistics. It also collects line-by-line information in a file cachegrind.out.<pid>, where <pid> is the program's process ID.

   Branch prediction statistics are not collected by default. To do so, add the flag --branch-sim=yes.

   This step should be done every time you want to collect information about a new program, a changed program, or about the same program with different input.

2. Generate a function-by-function summary, and possibly annotate source
   files, using the supplied cg_annotate program. Source files to annotate can
   be specified manually, or manually on the command line, or "interesting"
   source files can be annotated automatically with the --auto=yes option.
   You can annotate C/C++ files or assembly language files equally easily.

   This step can be performed as many times as you like for each Step 2. You
   may want to do multiple annotations showing different information each
   time.

As an optional intermediate step, you can use the supplied cg_merge program
to sum together the outputs of multiple Cachegrind runs, into a single file which
you then use as the input for cg_annotate.

These steps are described in detail in the following sections.

6.1.2 Cache simulation specifics

Cachegrind simulates a machine with independent first level instruction and
data caches (I1 and D1), backed by a unified second level cache (L2). This
configuration is used by almost all modern machines. Some old Cyrix CPUs
had a unified I and D L1 cache, but they are ancient history now.

Specific characteristics of the simulation are as follows:

- Write-allocate: when a write miss occurs, the block written to is brought
  into the D1 cache. Most modern caches have this property.

- Bit-selection hash function: the line(s) in the cache to which a memory
  block maps is chosen by the middle bits M–(M+N-1) of the byte address,
  where:

  - line size = 2^M bytes
  - (cache size / line size) = 2^N bytes

- Inclusive L2 cache: the L2 cache replicates all the entries of the L1 cache.
  This is standard on Pentium chips, but AMD Opterons, Athlons and
  Durons use an exclusive L2 cache that only holds blocks evicted from
  L1. Ditto most modern VIA CPUs.

The cache configuration simulated (cache size, associativity and line size) is
determined automagically using the CPUID instruction. If you have an old
machine that (a) doesn't support the CPUID instruction, or (b) supports it in
an early incarnation that doesn't give any cache information, then Cachegrind
will fall back to using a default configuration (that of a model 3/4 Athlon).
Cachegrind will tell you if this happens. You can manually specify one, two or
all three levels (I1/D1/L2) of the cache from the command line using the --I1,
--D1 and --L2 options.

On PowerPC platforms Cachegrind cannot automatically determine the cache
configuration, so you will need to specify it with the --I1, --D1 and --L2
options.

Other noteworthy behaviour:

- References that straddle two cache lines are treated as follows:

  - If both blocks hit ⇒ counted as one hit

- If one block hits, the other misses ⇒ counted as one miss.

- If both blocks miss ⇒ counted as one miss (not two)

- Instructions that modify a memory location (e.g. inc and dec) are counted as doing just a read, i.e. a single data reference. This may seem strange, but since the write can never cause a miss (the read guarantees the block is in the cache) it's not very interesting.

Thus it measures not the number of times the data cache is accessed, but the number of times a data cache miss could occur.

If you are interested in simulating a cache with different properties, it is not particularly hard to write your own cache simulator, or to modify the existing ones in vg_cachesim_I1.c, vg_cachesim_D1.c, vg_cachesim_L2.c and vg_cachesim_gen.c. We'd be interested to hear from anyone who does.

6.1.3 Branch simulation specifics

Cachegrind simulates branch predictors intended to be typical of mainstream desktop/server processors of around 2004.

Conditional branches are predicted using an array of 16,384 2-bit saturating counters. The array index used for a branch instruction is computed partly from the low-order bits of the branch instruction's address and partly using the taken/not-taken behaviour of the last few conditional branches. As a result the predictions for any specific branch depend both on its own history and the behaviour of previous branches. This is a standard technique for improving prediction accuracy.

For indirect branches (that is, jumps to unknown destinations) Cachegrind uses a simple branch target address predictor. Targets are predicted using an array of 512 entries indexed by the low order 9 bits of the branch instruction's address. Each branch is predicted to jump to the same address it did last time. Any other behaviour causes a mispredict.

More recent processors have better branch predictors, in particular better indirect branch predictors. Cachegrind's predictor design is deliberately conservative so as to be representative of the large installed base of processors which pre-date widespread deployment of more sophisticated indirect branch predictors. In particular, late model Pentium 4s (Prescott), Pentium M, Core and Core 2 have more sophisticated indirect branch predictors than modelled by Cachegrind.

Cachegrind does not simulate a return stack predictor. It assumes that processors perfectly predict function return addresses, an assumption which is probably close to being true.

See Hennessy and Patterson's classic text *Computer Architecture: A Quantitative Approach*, 4th edition (2007), Section 2.3 (pages 80-89) for background on modern branch predictors.

6.2 Profiling programs

To gather cache profiling information about the program ls -l, invoke
Cachegrind like this:

        valgrind --tool=cachegrind ls -l

The program will execute (slowly). Upon completion, summary statistics
that look like this will be printed:

        ==31751== I   refs: 27,742,716
        ==31751== I1   misses: 276
        ==31751== L2   misses: 275
        ==31751== I1   miss rate: 0.0%
        ==31751== L2i miss rate: 0.0%
        ==31751==
        ==31751== D   refs: 15,430,290 (10,955,517 rd +
                                                  4,474,773 wr)
        ==31751== D1   misses: 41,185 (21,905 rd +
                                                     19,280 wr)
        ==31751== L2   misses: 23,085 (3,987 rd +
                                                     19,098 wr)
        ==31751== D1   miss rate: 0.2% (0.1% +
                                                        0.4%)
        ==31751== L2d miss rate: 0.1% (0.0% +
                                                        0.4%)
        ==31751==
        ==31751== L2 misses: 23,360 (4,262 rd +
                                                     19,098 wr)
        ==31751== L2 miss rate: 0.0% (0.0% +
                                                        0.4%)

Cache accesses for instruction fetches are summarised first, giving the number
of fetches made (this is the number of instructions executed, which can be useful
to know in its own right), the number of I1 misses, and the number of L2
instruction (L2i) misses.

Cache accesses for data follow. The information is similar to that of the
instruction fetches, except that the values are also shown split between reads
and writes (note each row's rd and wr values add up to the row's total).

Combined instruction and data figures for the L2 cache follow that.

6.2.1 Output file

As well as printing summary information, Cachegrind also writes line-by-
line cache profiling information to a user-specified file. By default this file is
named cachegrind.out.<pid>. This file is human-readable, but is intended to
be interpreted by the accompanying program cg_annotate, described in the next
section.

Things to note about the cachegrind.out.<pid> file:

- It is written every time Cachegrind is run, and will overwrite any existing
  cachegrind.out.<pid> in the current directory (but that won't happen
  very often because it takes some time for process ids to be recycled).

- To use an output file name other than the default cachegrind.out, use the --cachegrind-out-file switch.

- It can be big: ls -l generates a file of about 350KB. Browsing a few files and web pages with a Konqueror built with full debugging information generates a file of around 15 MB.

The default .<pid> suffix on the output file name serves two purposes. Firstly, it means you don't have to rename old log files that you don't want to over-write. Secondly, and more importantly, it allows correct profiling with the --trace-children=yes option of programs that spawn child processes.

6.2.2 Cachegrind options

Using command line options, you can manually specify the I1/D1/L2 cache configuration to simulate. For each cache, you can specify the size, associativity and line size. The size and line size are measured in bytes. The three items must be comma-separated, but with no spaces, e.g.:

    valgrind --tool=cachegrind --I1=65535,2,64

You can specify one, two or three of the I1/D1/L2 caches. Any level not manually specified will be simulated using the configuration found in the normal way (via the CPUID instruction for automagic cache configuration, or failing that, via defaults).

Cache-simulation specific options are:

- --I1=<size>,<associativity>,<line size>

  Specify the size, associativity and line size of the level 1 instruction cache.

- --D1=<size>,<associativity>,<line size>

  Specify the size, associativity and line size of the level 1 data cache.

- --L2=<size>,<associativity>,<line size>

  Specify the size, associativity and line size of the level 2 cache.

- --cachegrind-out-file=<file>

  Write the profile data to file rather than to the default output file, cachegrind.out.<pid>. The %p and %q format specifiers can be used to embed the process ID and/or the contents of an environment variable in the name, as is the case for the core option --log-file. See Section 3.6.2 [Basic Options], page 18 for details.

- --cache-sim=no|yes [yes]

  Enables or disables collection of cache access and miss counts.

- --branch-sim=no|yes [no]

  Enables or disables collection of branch instruction and misprediction counts. By default this is disabled as it slows Cachegrind down by approximately 25%. Note that you cannot specify --cache-sim=no and --branch-sim=no together, as that would leave Cachegrind with no information to collect.

6.2.3 Annotating C/C++ programs

Before using cg_annotate, it is worth widening your window to be at least 120-characters wide if possible, as the output lines can be quite long.

To get a function-by-function summary, run `cg_annotate <filename>` on a Cachegrind output file.

The output looks like this:

```
-------------------------------------------------------
I1 cache:           65536 B, 64 B, 2-way associative
D1 cache:           65536 B, 64 B, 2-way associative
L2 cache:           262144 B, 64 B, 8-way associative
Command:            concord vg_to_ucode.c
Events recorded:  Ir I1mr I2mr Dr D1mr D2mr Dw D1mw D2mw
Events shown:     Ir I1mr I2mr Dr D1mr D2mr Dw D1mw D2mw
Event sort order: Ir I1mr I2mr Dr D1mr D2mr Dw D1mw D2mw
Threshold:          99%
Chosen for annotation:
Auto-annotation:    on


-------------------------------------------------------
Ir          I1mr I2mr Dr          D1mr   D2mr   Dw
   D1mw   D2mw
-------------------------------------------------------
27,742,716  276  275 10,955,517 21,905 3,987 4,474,773
   19,280 19,098  PROGRAM TOTALS


-------------------------------------------------------
Ir          I1mr I2mr Dr          D1mr   D2mr   Dw
   D1mw   D2mw  file:function
-------------------------------------------------------
8,821,482     5    5 2,242,702 1,621     73 1,794,230
       0      0  getc.c:_IO_getc
5,222,023     4    4 2,276,334    16     12   875,959
       1      1  concord.c:get_word
2,649,248     2    2 1,344,810 7,326  1,385         .
       .      .  vg_main.c:strcmp
2,521,927     2    2   591,215     0      0   179,398
       0      0  concord.c:hash
2,242,740     2    2 1,046,612   568     22   448,548
       0      0  ctype.c:tolower
1,496,937     4    4   630,874 9,000  1,400   279,388
       0      0  concord.c:insert
  897,991    51   51   897,831    95     30        62
       1      1  ???:???
  598,068     1    1   299,034     0      0   149,517
       0      0  lockfile.c:__flockfile
  598,068     0    0   299,034     0      0   149,517
       0      0  lockfile.c:__funlockfile
```

```
598,024      4    4    213,580     35     16     149,506
     0       0    vg_clientmalloc.c:malloc
446,587      1    1    215,973  2,167    430     129,948
14,057  13,957    concord.c:add_existing
341,760      2    2    128,160      0      0     128,160
     0       0    vg_clientmalloc.c:vg_trap_here_WRAPPER
320,782      4    4    150,711    276      0      56,027
    53      53    concord.c:init_hash_table
298,998      1    1    106,785      0      0      64,071
     1       1    concord.c:create
149,518      0    0    149,516      0      0           1
     0       0    ???:tolower@@GLIBC_2.0
149,518      0    0    149,516      0      0           1
     0       0    ???:fgetc@@GLIBC_2.0
95,983       4    4     38,031      0      0      34,409
3,152   3,150    concord.c:new_word_node
85,440       0    0     42,720      0      0      21,360
     0       0    vg_clientmalloc.c:vg_bogus_epilogue
```

First up is a summary of the annotation options:

- I1 cache, D1 cache, L2 cache: cache configuration. So you know the configuration with which these results were obtained.

- Command: the command line invocation of the program under examination.

- Events recorded: event abbreviations are:
  - Ir: I cache reads (i.e. instructions executed)
  - I1mr: I1 cache read misses
  - I2mr: L2 cache instruction read misses
  - Dr: D cache reads (i.e. memory reads)
  - D1mr: D1 cache read misses
  - D2mr: L2 cache data read misses
  - Dw: D cache writes (i.e. memory writes)
  - D1mw: D1 cache write misses
  - D2mw: L2 cache data write misses
  - Bc: Conditional branches executed
  - Bcm: Conditional branches mispredicted
  - Bi: Indirect branches executed
  - Bim: Conditional branches mispredicted

Note that D1 total accesses is given by D1mr + D1mw, and that L2 total accesses is given by I2mr + D2mr + D2mw.

- Events shown: the events shown, which is a subset of the events gathered. This can be adjusted with the --show option.

- Event sort order: the sort order in which functions are shown. For example, in this case the functions are sorted from highest Ir counts to lowest. If two functions have identical Ir counts, they will then be sorted by I1mr counts, and so on. This order can be adjusted with the --sort option.

  Note that this dictates the order the functions appear. It is not the order in which the columns appear; that is dictated by the "events shown" line (and can be changed with the --show option).

- Threshold: cg_annotate by default omits functions that cause very low counts to avoid drowning you in information. In this case, cg_annotate shows summaries the functions that account for 99% of the Ir counts; Ir is chosen as the threshold event since it is the primary sort event. The threshold can be adjusted with the --threshold option.

- Chosen for annotation: names of files specified manually for annotation; in this case none.

- Auto-annotation: whether auto-annotation was requested via the --auto=yes option. In this case no.

Then follows summary statistics for the whole program. These are similar to the summary provided when running valgrind --tool=cachegrind.

Then follows function-by-function statistics. Each function is identified by a file_name:function_name pair. If a column contains only a dot it means the function never performs that event (e.g. the third row shows that strcmp() contains no instructions that write to memory). The name ??? is used if the the file name and/or function name could not be determined from debugging information. If most of the entries have the form ???:??? the program probably wasn't compiled with -g. If any code was invalidated (either due to self-modifying code or unloading of shared objects) its counts are aggregated into a single cost centre written as (discarded):(discarded).

It is worth noting that functions will come both from the profiled program (e.g. 'concord.c') and from libraries (e.g. 'getc.c')

There are two ways to annotate source files—by choosing them manually, or with the --auto=yes option. To do it manually, just specify the filenames as additional arguments to cg_annotate. For example, the output from running 'cg_annotate <filename> concord.c' for our example produces the same output as above followed by an annotated version of 'concord.c', a section of which looks like:

```
----------------------------------------------------------
-- User-annotated source: concord.c
----------------------------------------------------------

Ir          I1mr I2mr Dr      D1mr D2mr  Dw   D1mw    D2mw


   .     .    .      .     .     .     .      .      .
void init_hash_table(char *file_name, Word_Node *table[])
   3     1    1      .     .     .     1      0      0
   {
   .     .    .      .     .     .     .      .      .

       FILE *file_ptr;
```

```
          .      .      .        .        .        .        .        .        .
              Word_Info *data;
      1       0      0        .        .        .        1        1        1
              int line = 1, i;
          .      .      .        .        .        .        .        .        .
      5       0      0        .        .        .        3        0        0
              data = (Word_Info *) create(sizeof(Word_Info));
          .      .      .        .        .        .        .        .        .
  4,991       0      0    1,995        0        0      998        0        0
              for (i = 0; i < TABLE_SIZE; i++)
  3,988       1      1    1,994        0        0      997       53       52
                  table[i] = NULL;
          .      .      .        .        .        .        .        .        .

          .      .      .        .        .        .        .        .        .
              /* Open file, check it. */
      6       0      0        1        0        0        4        0        0
              file_ptr = fopen(file_name, "r");
      2       0      0        1        0        0        .        .        .
              if (!(file_ptr)) {
          .      .      .        .        .        .        .        .        .
                  fprintf(stderr, "Couldn't open '%s'.\n",
                          file_name);
      1       1      1        .        .        .        .        .        .
                  exit(EXIT_FAILURE);
          .      .      .        .        .        .        .        .        .
              }
          .      .      .        .        .        .        .        .        .
165,062       1      1   73,360        0        0   91,700        0        0
              while ((line = get_word(data, line, file_ptr)) != EOF)
146,712       0      0   73,356        0        0   73,356        0        0
                  insert(data->;word, data->line, table);
          .      .      .        .        .        .        .        .        .
      4       0      0        1        0        0        2        0        0
              free(data);
      4       0      0        1        0        0        2        0        0
              fclose(file_ptr);
      3       0      0        2        0        0        .        .        .
          }
```

(Although column widths are automatically minimised, a wide terminal is clearly useful.)

Each source file is clearly marked (User-annotated source) as having been chosen manually for annotation. If the file was found in one of the directories specified with the -I / --include option, the directory and file are both given.

Each line is annotated with its event counts. Events not applicable for a line are represented by a dot. This is useful for distinguishing between an event which cannot happen, and one which can but did not.

Sometimes only a small section of a source file is executed. To minimise uninteresting output, Cachegrind only shows annotated lines and lines within a small distance of annotated lines. Gaps are marked with the line numbers so you know which part of a file the shown code comes from, e.g.:

```
(figures and code for line 704)
-- line 704 ----------------------------------------
-- line 878 ----------------------------------------
(figures and code for line 878)
```

The amount of context to show around annotated lines is controlled by the --context option.

To get automatic annotation, run cg_annotate <filename> --auto=yes. cg_annotate will automatically annotate every source file it can find that is mentioned in the function-by-function summary. Therefore, the files chosen for auto-annotation are affected by the --sort and --threshold options. Each source file is clearly marked (Auto-annotated source) as being chosen automatically. Any files that could not be found are mentioned at the end of the output, e.g.:

```
----------------------------------------------------
The following files chosen for auto-annotation could
not be found:
----------------------------------------------------
  getc.c
  ctype.c
  ../sysdeps/generic/lockfile.c
```

This is quite common for library files, since libraries are usually compiled with debugging information, but the source files are often not present on a system. If a file is chosen for annotation both manually and automatically, it is marked as User-annotated source. Use the -I / --include option to tell Valgrind where to look for source files if the filenames found from the debugging information aren't specific enough.

Beware that cg_annotate can take some time to digest large cachegrind.out.<pid> files, e.g. 30 seconds or more. Also beware that auto-annotation can produce a lot of output if your program is large!

6.2.4 Annotating assembly code programs

Valgrind can annotate assembly code programs too, or annotate the assembly code generated for your C program. Sometimes this is useful for understanding what is really happening when an interesting line of C code is translated into multiple instructions.

To do this, you just need to assemble your .s files with assembler-level debug information. gcc doesn't do this, but you can use the GNU assembler with the --gstabs option to generate object files with this information, e.g.:

```
as --gstabs foo.s
```

You can then profile and annotate source files in the same way as for C/C++ programs.

6.3 cg_annotate options

- -h, --help

  -v, --version

  Help and version, as usual.

- --sort=A,B,C [default: order in cachegrind.out.<pid>]

  Specifies the events upon which the sorting of the function-by-function entries will be based. Useful if you want to concentrate on e.g. I cache misses (--sort=I1mr,I2mr), or D cache misses (--sort=D1mr,D2mr), or L2 misses (--sort=D2mr,I2mr).

- --show=A,B,C [default: all, order from cachegrind.out.<pid>]

  Specifies which events to show (and the column order). Default is to use all present in the cachegrind.out.<pid> file (and use the order in the file).

- --threshold=X [default: 99%]

  Sets the threshold for the function-by-function summary. Functions are shown that account for more than X% of the primary sort event. If auto-annotating, also affects which files are annotated.

  Note: thresholds can be set for more than one of the events by appending any events for the --sort option with a colon and a number (no spaces, though). E.g. if you want to see the functions that cover 99% of L2 read misses and 99% of L2 write misses, use this option:

  --sort=D2mr:99,D2mw:99

- --auto=no [default]

  --auto=yes

  When enabled, automatically annotates every file that is mentioned in the function-by-function summary that can be found. Also gives a list of those that couldn't be found.

- --context=N [default: 8]

  Print N lines of context before and after each annotated line. Avoids printing large sections of source files that were not executed. Use a large number (e.g. 10,000) to show all source lines.

- -I<dir>, --include=<dir> [default: empty string]

  Adds a directory to the list in which to search for files. Multiple -I/-include options can be given to add multiple directories.

6.3.1 Warnings

There are a couple of situations in which cg_annotate issues warnings.

- If a source file is more recent than the cachegrind.out.<pid> file. This is
  because the information in cachegrind.out.<pid> is only recorded with
  line numbers, so if the line numbers change at all in the source (e.g. lines
  added, deleted, swapped), any annotations will be incorrect.

- If information is recorded about line numbers past the end of a file. This
  can be caused by the above problem, i.e. shortening the source file while
  using an old cachegrind.out.<pid> file. If this happens, the figures for
  the bogus lines are printed anyway (clearly marked as bogus) in case they
  are important.

6.3.2 Things to watch out for

Some odd things that can occur during annotation:

- If annotating at the assembler level, you might see something like this:

```
1 0 0   . . .   . . .        leal -12(%ebp),%eax
1 0 0   . . .   1 0 0        movl %eax,84(%ebx)
2 0 0   0 0 0   1 0 0        movl $1,-20(%ebp)
. . .   . . .   . . .        .align 4,0x90
1 0 0   . . .   . . .        movl $.LnrB,%eax
1 0 0   . . .   1 0 0        movl %eax,-16(%ebp)
```

How can the third instruction be executed twice when the others are executed only once? As it turns out, it isn't. Here's a dump of the executable,
using objdump -d:

```
8048f25: 8d 45 f4          lea 0xfffffff4(%ebp),%eax
8048f28: 89 43 54          mov %eax,0x54(%ebx)
8048f2b: c7 45 ec 01 ...   movl $0x1,0xffffffec(%ebp)
8048f32: 89 f6             mov %esi,%esi
8048f34: b8 08 8b 07 08    mov $0x8078b08,%eax
8048f39: 89 45 f0          mov %eax,0xfffffff0(%ebp)
```

Notice the extra mov %esi,%esi instruction. Where did this come from?
The GNU assembler inserted it to serve as the two bytes of padding needed
to align the movl $.LnrB,%eax instruction on a four-byte boundary, but
pretended it didn't exist when adding debug information. Thus when Valgrind reads the debug info it thinks that the movl $0x1,0xffffffec(%ebp)
instruction covers the address range 0x8048f2b–0x804833 by itself, and at-
tributes the counts for the mov %esi,%esi to it.

- Inlined functions can cause strange results in the function-by-function
  summary. If a function inline_me() is defined in 'foo.h' and inlined
  in the functions f1(), f2() and f3() in 'bar.c', there will not be
  a foo.h:inline_me() function entry. Instead, there will be separate
  function entries for each inlining site, i.e. foo.h:f1(), foo.h:f2() and
  foo.h:f3(). To find the total counts for foo.h:inline_me(), add up the
  counts from each entry.

The reason for this is that although the debug info output by gcc indicates the switch from 'bar.c' to 'foo.h', it doesn't indicate the name of the function in 'foo.h', so Valgrind keeps using the old one.

- Sometimes, the same filename might be represented with a relative name and with an absolute name in different parts of the debug info, e.g.: '/home/user/proj/proj.h' and '../proj.h'. In this case, if you use auto-annotation, the file will be annotated twice with the counts split between the two.

- Files with more than 65,535 lines cause difficulties for the Stabs-format debug info reader. This is because the line number in the struct nlist defined in 'a.out.h' under Linux is only a 16-bit value. Valgrind can handle some files with more than 65,535 lines correctly by making some guesses to identify line number overflows. But some cases are beyond it, in which case you'll get a warning message explaining that annotations for the file might be incorrect.

  If you are using gcc 3.1 or later, this is most likely irrelevant, since gcc switched to using the more modern DWARF2 format by default at version 3.1. DWARF2 does not have any such limitations on line numbers.

- If you compile some files with -g and some without, some events that take place in a file without debug info could be attributed to the last line of a file with debug info (whichever one gets placed before the non-debug-info file in the executable).

This list looks long, but these cases should be fairly rare.

6.3.3 Accuracy

Valgrind's cache profiling has a number of shortcomings:

- It doesn't account for kernel activity—the effect of system calls on the cache contents is ignored.

- It doesn't account for other process activity. This is probably desirable when considering a single program.

- It doesn't account for virtual-to-physical address mappings. Hence the simulation is not a true representation of what's happening in the cache. Most caches are physically indexed, but Cachegrind simulates caches using virtual addresses.

- It doesn't account for cache misses not visible at the instruction level, e.g. those arising from TLB misses, or speculative execution.

- Valgrind will schedule threads differently from how they would be when running natively. This could warp the results for threaded programs.

- The x86/amd64 instructions bts, btr and btc will incorrectly be counted as doing a data read if both the arguments are registers, e.g.:

      btsl %eax, %edx

This should only happen rarely.

- x86/amd64 FPU instructions with data sizes of 28 and 108 bytes (e.g. fsave) are treated as though they only access 16 bytes. These instructions seem to be rare so hopefully this won't affect accuracy much.

Another thing worth noting is that results are very sensitive. Changing the size of the the executable being profiled, or the sizes of any of the shared libraries it uses, or even the length of their file names, can perturb the results. Variations will be small, but don't expect perfectly repeatable results if your program changes at all.

More recent GNU/Linux distributions do address space randomisation, in which identical runs of the same program have their shared libraries loaded at different locations, as a security measure. This also perturbs the results.

While these factors mean you shouldn't trust the results to be super-accurate, hopefully they should be close enough to be useful.

6.4 Merging profiles with cg_merge

cg_merge is a simple program which reads multiple profile files, as created by cachegrind, merges them together, and writes the results into another file in the same format. You can then examine the merged results using cg_annotate <filename>, as described above. The merging functionality might be useful if you want to aggregate costs over multiple runs of the same program, or from a single parallel run with multiple instances of the same program.

cg_merge is invoked as follows:

```
cg_merge -o outputfile file1 file2 file3 ...
```

It reads and checks file1, then read and checks file2 and merges it into the running totals, then the same with file3, etc. The final results are written to outputfile, or to standard out if no output file is specified.

Costs are summed on a per-function, per-line and per-instruction basis. Because of this, the order in which the input files does not matter, although you should take care to only mention each file once, since any file mentioned twice will be added in twice.

cg_merge does not attempt to check that the input files come from runs of the same executable. It will happily merge together profile files from completely unrelated programs. It does however check that the Events: lines of all the inputs are identical, so as to ensure that the addition of costs makes sense. For example, it would be nonsensical for it to add a number indicating D1 read references to a number from a different file indicating L2 write misses.

A number of other syntax and sanity checks are done whilst reading the inputs. cg_merge will stop and attempt to print a helpful error message if any of the input files fail these checks.

6.5 Acting on Cachegrind's information

So, you've managed to profile your program with Cachegrind. Now what? What's the best way to actually act on the information it provides to speed up your program? Here are some rules of thumb that we have found to be useful.

First of all, the global hit/miss rate numbers are not that useful. If you have multiple programs or multiple runs of a program, comparing the numbers might identify if any are outliers and worthy of closer investigation. Otherwise, they're not enough to act on.

The line-by-line source code annotations are much more useful. In our experience, the best place to start is by looking at the Ir numbers. They simply measure how many instructions were executed for each line, and don't include any cache information, but they can still be very useful for identifying bottlenecks.

After that, we have found that L2 misses are typically a much bigger source of slow-downs than L1 misses. So it's worth looking for any snippets of code that cause a high proportion of the L2 misses. If you find any, it's still not always easy to work out how to improve things. You need to have a reasonable understanding of how caches work, the principles of locality, and your program's data access patterns. Improving things may require redesigning a data structure, for example.

In short, Cachegrind can tell you where some of the bottlenecks in your code are, but it can't tell you how to fix them. You have to work that out for yourself. But at least you have the information!

6.6 Implementation details

This section talks about details you don't need to know about in order to use Cachegrind, but may be of interest to some people.

6.6.1 How Cachegrind works

The best reference for understanding how Cachegrind works is chapter 3 of *Dynamic Binary Analysis and Instrumentation*, by Nicholas Nethercote. It is available on the Valgrind publications page.

6.6.2 Cachegrind output file format

The file format is fairly straightforward, basically giving the cost centre for every line, grouped by files and functions. Total counts (e.g. total cache accesses, total L1 misses) are calculated when traversing this structure rather than during execution, to save time; the cache simulation functions are called so often that even one or two extra adds can make a sizeable difference.

The file format:

```
file          ::= desc_line* cmd_line events_line
                  data_line+ summary_line
desc_line     ::= "desc:" ws? non_nl_string
cmd_line      ::= "cmd:" ws? cmd
events_line   ::= "events:" ws? (event ws)+
data_line     ::= file_line | fn_line | count_line
```

```
file_line     ::= "fl=" filename
fn_line       ::= "fn=" fn_name
count_line    ::= line_num ws? (count ws)+
summary_line  ::= "summary:" ws? (count ws)+
count         ::= num | "."
```

Where:

- `non_nl_string` is any string not containing a newline.
- `cmd` is a string holding the command line of the profiled program.
- `event` is a string containing no whitespace.
- `filename` and `fn_name` are strings.
- `num` and `line_num` are decimal numbers.
- `ws` is whitespace.

The contents of the `desc:` lines are printed out at the top of the summary. This is a generic way of providing simulation specific information, e.g. for giving the cache configuration for cache simulation.

More than one line of info can be presented for each file/fn/line number. In such cases, the counts for the named events will be accumulated.

Counts can be . to represent zero. This makes the files easier for humans to read.

The number of counts in each `line` and the `summary_line` should not exceed the number of events in the `event_line`. If the number in each `line` is less, cg_annotate treats those missing as though they were a . entry. This saves space.

A `file_line` changes the current file name. A `fn_line` changes the current function name. A `count_line` contains counts that pertain to the current filename/fn_name. A `fn=` `file_line` and a `fn_line` must appear before any `count_lines` to give the context of the first `count_lines`.

Each `file_line` will normally be immediately followed by a `fn_line`. But it doesn't have to be.

7 Callgrind: a call graph profiler

Callgrind is a profiling tool that can construct a call graph for a program's run. By default, the collected data consists of the number of instructions executed, their relationship to source lines, the caller/callee relationship between functions, and the numbers of such calls. Optionally, a cache simulator (similar to cachegrind) can produce further information about the memory access behavior of the application.

The profile data is written out to a file at program termination. For presentation of the data, and interactive control of the profiling, two command line tools are provided:

- `callgrind_annotate` This command reads in the profile data, and prints a sorted lists of functions, optionally with source annotation.

  For graphical visualization of the data, try KCachegrind, which is a KDE/Qt based GUI that makes it easy to navigate the large amount of data that Callgrind produces.

- `callgrind_control` This command enables you to interactively observe and control the status of currently running applications, without stopping the application. You can get statistics information as well as the current stack trace, and you can request zeroing of counters or dumping of profile data.

To use Callgrind, you must specify `--tool=callgrind` on the Valgrind command line.

7.1 Functionality

Cachegrind collects flat profile data: event counts (data reads, cache misses, etc.) are attributed directly to the function they occurred in. This cost attribution mechanism is called *self* or *exclusive* attribution.

Callgrind extends this functionality by propagating costs across function call boundaries. If function `foo` calls `bar`, the costs from `bar` are added into `foo`'s costs. When applied to the program as a whole, this builds up a picture of so called *inclusive* costs, that is, where the cost of each function includes the costs of all functions it called, directly or indirectly.

As an example, the inclusive cost of `main` should be almost 100 percent of the total program cost. Because of costs arising before `main` is run, such as initialization of the run time linker and construction of global C++ objects, the inclusive cost of `main` is not exactly 100 percent of the total program cost.

Together with the call graph, this allows you to find the specific call chains starting from `main` in which the majority of the program's costs occur. Caller/callee cost attribution is also useful for profiling functions called from multiple call sites, and where optimization opportunities depend on changing code in the callers, in particular by reducing the call count.

Callgrind's cache simulation is based on the Cachegrind tool. Read Cachegrind's documentation first. The material below describes the features supported in addition to Cachegrind's features.

Callgrind's ability to detect function calls and returns depends on the instruction set of the platform it is run on. It works best on x86 and amd64, and unfortunately currently does not work so well on PowerPC code. This is because there are no explicit call or return instructions in the PowerPC instruction set, so Callgrind has to rely on heuristics to detect calls and returns.

7.2 Basic Usage

As with Cachegrind, you probably want to compile with debugging info (the -g flag), but with optimization turned on.

To start a profile run for a program, execute:

```
valgrind --tool=callgrind [callgrind options] your-program
    [your options]
```

While the simulation is running, you can observe execution with

```
callgrind_control -b
```

This will print out the current backtrace. To annotate the backtrace with event counts, run

```
callgrind_control -e -b
```

After program termination, Callgrind generates a profile data file named callgrind.out.<pid>, where *pid* is the process ID of the program being profiled. The data file contains information about the calls made in the program among the functions executed, together with events of type Instruction Read Accesses (Ir).

To generate a function-by-function summary from the profile data file, use

```
callgrind_annotate [options] callgrind.out.<pid>
```

This summary is similar to the output you get from a Cachegrind run with cg_annotate: the list of functions is ordered by exclusive cost of functions, which also are the ones that are shown. Important for the additional features of Callgrind are the following two options:

- --inclusive=yes: Instead of using exclusive cost of functions as sorting order, use and show inclusive cost.

- --tree=both: Interleave into the top level list of functions, information on the callers and the callees of each function. In these lines, which represents executed calls, the cost gives the number of events spent in the call. Indented, above each function, there is the list of callers, and below, the list of callees. The sum of events in calls to a given function (caller lines), as well as the sum of events in calls from the function (callee lines) together with the self cost, gives the total inclusive cost of the function.

Use --auto=yes to get annotated source code for all relevant functions for which the source can be found. In addition to source annotation as produced by cg_annotate, you will see the annotated call sites with call counts. For all other options, consult the (Cachegrind) documentation for cg_annotate.

For better call graph browsing experience, it is highly recommended to use KCachegrind. If your code has a significant fraction of its cost in *cycles* (sets of functions calling each other in a recursive manner), you have to use KCachegrind, as `callgrind_annotate` currently does not do any cycle detection, which is important to get correct results in this case.

If you are additionally interested in measuring the cache behavior of your program, use Callgrind with the option `--simulate-cache=yes`. However, expect a further slow down approximately by a factor of 2.

If the program section you want to profile is somewhere in the middle of the run, it is beneficial to *fast forward* to this section without any profiling, and then switch on profiling. This is achieved by using the command line option `--instr-atstart=no` and running, in a shell, `callgrind_control -i` on just before the interesting code section is executed. To exactly specify the code position where profiling should start, use the client request `CALLGRIND_START_INSTRUMENTATION`.

If you want to be able to see assembly code level annotation, specify `--dump-instr=yes`. This will produce profile data at instruction granularity. Note that the resulting profile data can only be viewed with KCachegrind. For assembly annotation, it also is interesting to see more details of the control flow inside of functions, i.e. (conditional) jumps. This will be collected by further specifying `--collect-jumps=yes`.

7.3 Advanced Usage

7.3.1 Multiple profiling dumps from one program run

Sometimes you are not interested in characteristics of a full program run, but only of a small part of it, for example execution of one algorithm. If there are multiple algorithms, or one algorithm running with different input data, it may even be useful to get different profile information for different parts of a single program run.

Profile data files have names of the form

    callgrind.out.pid.part-threadID

where *pid* is the PID of the running program, *part* is a number incremented on each dump ('.part' is skipped for the dump at program termination), and *threadID* is a thread identification ('-threadID' is only used if you request dumps of individual threads with `--separate-threads=yes`).

There are different ways to generate multiple profile dumps while a program is running under Callgrind's supervision. Nevertheless, all methods trigger the same action, which is "dump all profile information since the last dump or program start, and zero cost counters afterwards". To allow for zeroing cost counters without dumping, there is a second action "zero all cost counters now". The different methods are:

- **Dump on program termination.** This method is the standard way and doesn't need any special action on your part.

- **Spontaneous, interactive dumping.** Use

`callgrind_control -d [hint [PID/Name]]`

to request the dumping of profile information of the supervised application
with PID or Name. *hint* is an arbitrary string you can optionally specify
to later be able to distinguish profile dumps. The control program will not
terminate before the dump is completely written. Note that the application must be actively running for detection of the dump command. So,
for a GUI application, resize the window, or for a server, send a request.

If you are using KCachegrind for browsing of profile information, you can
use the toolbar button Force dump. This will request a dump and trigger
a reload after the dump is written.

- Periodic dumping after execution of a specified number of basic
  blocks.

  For this, use the command line option --dump-every-bb=count.

- Dumping at enter/leave of specified functions.

  Use the option --dump-before=*func* and --dump-after=*func*. To zero
  cost counters before entering a function, use --zero-before=*func*.

  You can specify these options multiple times for different functions. Function specifications support wildcards: e.g. use --dump-before='foo*' to
  generate dumps before entering any function starting with *foo*.

- Program controlled dumping. Put

  `#include <valgrind/callgrind.h>`

  into your source and add CALLGRIND_DUMP_STATS; when you want a dump
  to happen. Use CALLGRIND_ZERO_STATS; to only zero cost centers.

  In Valgrind terminology, this method is called "Client requests". The given
  macros generate a special instruction pattern with no effect at all (i.e.
  a NOP). When run under Valgrind, the CPU simulation engine detects
  the special instruction pattern and triggers special actions like the ones
  described above.

If you are running a multi-threaded application and specify the command line
option --separate-threads=yes, every thread will be profiled on its own and
will create its own profile dump. Thus, the last two methods will only generate
one dump of the currently running thread. With the other methods, you will
get multiple dumps (one for each thread) on a dump request.

7.3.2 Limiting the range of collected events

For aggregating events (function enter/leave, instruction execution, memory
access) into event numbers, first, the events must be recognizable by Callgrind,
and second, the collection state must be switched on.

Event collection is only possible if *instrumentation* for program code is
switched on. This is the default, but for faster execution (identical to valgrind
--tool=none), it can be switched off until the program reaches a state in which
you want to start collecting profiling data. Callgrind can start without instrumentation by specifying option --instr-atstart=no. Instrumentation can be
switched on interactively with

```
callgrind_control -i on
```
and off by specifying "off" instead of "on". Furthermore, instrumentation state can be programmatically changed with the macros CALLGRIND_START_ INSTRUMENTATION; and CALLGRIND_STOP_INSTRUMENTATION;.

In addition to enabling instrumentation, you must also enable event collection for the parts of your program you are interested in. By default, event collection is enabled everywhere. You can limit collection to a specific function by using --toggle-collect=function. This will toggle the collection state on entering and leaving the specified functions. When this option is in effect, the default collection state at program start is "off". Only events happening while running inside of the given function will be collected. Recursive calls of the given function do not trigger any action.

It is important to note that with instrumentation switched off, the cache simulator cannot see any memory access events, and thus, any simulated cache state will be frozen and wrong without instrumentation. Therefore, to get useful cache events (hits/misses) after switching on instrumentation, the cache first must warm up, probably leading to many *cold misses* which would not have happened in reality. If you do not want to see these, start event collection a few million instructions after you have switched on instrumentation.

7.3.3 Avoiding cycles

Informally speaking, a cycle is a group of functions which call each other in a recursive way.

Formally speaking, a cycle is a nonempty set S of functions, such that for every pair of functions F and G in S, it is possible to call from F to G (possibly via intermediate functions) and also from G to F. Furthermore, S must be maximal—that is, be the largest set of functions satisfying this property. For example, if a third function H is called from inside S and calls back into S, then H is also part of the cycle and should be included in S.

Recursion is quite usual in programs, and therefore, cycles sometimes appear in the call graph output of Callgrind. However, the title of this chapter should raise two questions: What is bad about cycles which makes you want to avoid them? And: How can cycles be avoided without changing program code?

Cycles are not bad in themselves, but tend to make performance analysis of your code harder. This is because inclusive costs for calls inside a cycle are meaningless. The definition of inclusive cost, i.e. self cost of a function plus inclusive cost of its callees, needs a topological order among functions. For cycles, this does not hold true: callees of a function in a cycle include the function itself. Therefore, KCachegrind does cycle detection and skips visualization of any inclusive cost for calls inside of cycles. Further, all functions in a cycle are collapsed into artifical functions called like Cycle 1.

Now, when a program exposes really big cycles (as is true for some GUI code, or in general code using event or callback based programming style), you lose the nice property of pinpointing the bottlenecks by following call chains from main(), guided via inclusive cost. In addition, KCachegrind loses its ability to show interesting parts of the call graph, as it uses inclusive costs to cut off uninteresting areas.

Despite the meaningless of inclusive costs in cycles, the need for some kind of visualization motivates the possibility of temporarily disabling cycle detection in KCachegrind. This can lead to a misguided visualization. However, often cycles appear because of an unlucky superposition of independent call chains in a way that the profile result will see a cycle. Neglecting calls with very small measured inclusive cost can break these cycles. In such cases, the incorrect handling of cycles (by not detecting them still) gives a meaningful profiling visualization.

It has to be noted that currently, `callgrind_annotate` does not do any cycle detection at all. For program executions with function recursion, it can print inclusive costs above 100%.

After describing why cycles are bad for profiling, it is worth talking about cycle avoidance. The key insight here is that symbols in the profile data do not have to exactly match the symbols found in the program. Instead, the symbol name could encode additional information from the current execution context such as recursion level of the current function, or even some part of the call chain leading to the function. While encoding of additional information into symbols is quite capable of avoiding cycles, it has to be used carefully to not cause symbol explosion. The latter imposes large memory requirement for Callgrind with possible out-of-memory conditions, and big profile data files.

Another way of avoiding cycles in Callgrind's profile data output is to leave out selected functions in the call graph. Of course, this also skips any call information from and to an ignored function, and thus can break a cycle. Candidates for this typically are dispatcher functions in event driven code. The option to ignore calls to a function is `--fn-skip=function`. Aside from possibly breaking cycles, this is used in Callgrind to skip trampoline functions in the PLT sections for calls to functions in shared libraries. You can see the difference if you profile with `--skip-plt=no`. If a call is ignored, its cost events will be propagated to the enclosing function.

If you have a recursive function, you can distinguish the first 10 recursion levels by specifying `--separate-recs10=function`. Or for all functions with `--separate-recs=10`, but this will give you much bigger profile data files. In the profile data, you will see the recursion levels of `func` as the different functions with names `func`, `func'2`, `func'3` and so on.

If you have call chains "A > B > C" and "A > C > B" in your program, you usually get a "false" cycle "B <> C". Use `--separate-callers2=B` `--separate-callers2=C`, and functions B and C will be treated as different functions depending on the direct caller. Using the apostrophe for appending this "context" to the function name, you get "A > B'A > C'B" and "A > C'A > B'C", and there will be no cycle. Use `--separate-callers=2` to get a 2-caller dependency for all functions. Note that doing this will increase the size of profile data files.

7.4 Command line option reference

In the following, options are grouped into classes, in the same order as the output of `callgrind --help`.

Some options allow the specification of a function/symbol name, such as `--dump-before=function`, or `--fn-skip=function`. All these options can be specified multiple times for different functions. In addition, the function specifications actually are patterns supporting the use of wildcards * (zero or more arbitrary characters) and ? (exactly one arbitrary character), similar to file name globbing in the shell. This feature is important especially for C++, as without wildcard usage the function would have to be specified in full extent, including parameter signature.

7.4.1 Miscellaneous options

- `--help` Show summary of options. This is a short version of this manual section.

- `--version` Show version of callgrind.

7.4.2 Dump creation options

These options influence the name and format of the profile data files.

- `--callgrind-out-file=<file>`

  Write the profile data to `file` rather than to the default output file, `callgrind.out.<pid>`. The `%p` and `%q` format specifiers can be used to embed the process ID and/or the contents of an environment variable in the name, as is the case for the core option `--log-file`. See Section 3.6.2 [Basic Options], page 18 for details. When multiple dumps are made, the file name is modified further; see below.

- `--dump-instr=<no|yes>` [default: no]

  This specifies that event counting should be performed at per-instruction granularity. This allows for assembly code annotation. Currently the results can only be displayed by KCachegrind.

- `--dump-line=<no|yes>` [default: yes]

  This specifies that event counting should be performed at source line granularity. This allows source annotation for sources which are compiled with debug information (-g).

- `--compress-strings=<no|yes>` [default: yes]

  This option influences the output format of the profile data. It specifies whether strings (file and function names) should be identified by numbers. This shrinks the file, but makes it more difficult for humans to read (which is not recommended in any case).

- `--compress-pos=<no|yes>` [default: yes]

  This option influences the output format of the profile data. It specifies whether numerical positions are always specified as absolute values or are allowed to be relative to previous numbers. This shrinks the file size,

- `--combine-dumps=<no|yes>` [default: no]

  When multiple profile data parts are to be generated, these parts are appended to the same output file if this option is set to "yes". Not recommended.

7.4.3 Activity options

These options specify when actions relating to event counts are to be executed. For interactive control use `callgrind_control`.

- `--dump-every-bb=<count>` [default: 0, never]

  Dump profile data every `<count>` basic blocks. Whether a dump is needed is only checked when Valgrind's internal scheduler is run. Therefore, the minimum useful setting is about 100000. The count is a 64-bit value to make long dump periods possible.

- `--dump-before=<function>`

  Dump when entering `<function>`

- `--zero-before=<function>`

  Zero all costs when entering `<function>`

- `--dump-after=<function>`

  Dump when leaving `<function>`

7.4.4 Data collection options

These options specify when events are to be aggregated into event counts. Also see Section 7.3.2 [Limiting range of event collection], page 82.

- `--instr-atstart=<yes|no>` [default: yes]

  Specify if you want Callgrind to start simulation and profiling from the beginning of the program. When set to no, Callgrind will not be able to collect any information, including calls, but it will have at most a slowdown of around 4, which is the minimum Valgrind overhead. Instrumentation can be interactively switched on via `callgrind_control -i on`.

  Note that the resulting call graph will most probably not contain main, but will contain all the functions executed after instrumentation was switched on. Instrumentation can also programatically switched on/off. See the Callgrind include file `<callgrind.h>` for the macro you have to use in your source code.

  For cache simulation, results will be less accurate when switching on instrumentation later in the program run, as the simulator starts with an empty cache at that moment. Switch on event collection later to cope with this error.

- `--collect-atstart=<yes|no>` [default: yes]   Specify whether event collection is switched on at beginning of the profile run.

  To only look at parts of your program, you have two possibilities:

1. Zero event counters before entering the program part you want to profile, and dump the event counters to a file after leaving that program part.

2. Switch on/off collection state as needed to only see event counters happening while inside of the program part you want to profile.

The second option can be used if the program part you want to profile is called many times. Option 1, i.e. creating a lot of dumps is not practical here.

Collection state can be toggled at entry and exit of a given function with the option `--toggle-collect`. If you use this flag, collection state should be switched off at the beginning. Note that the specification of `--toggle-collect` implicitly sets `--collect-state=no`.

Collection state can be toggled also by using a Valgrind Client Request in your application. For this, include `valgrind/callgrind.h` and specify the macro `CALLGRIND_TOGGLE_COLLECT` at the needed positions. This only will have any effect if run under supervision of the Callgrind tool.

- `--toggle-collect=<function>`

  Toggle collection on entry/exit of <function>.

- `--collect-jumps=<no|yes> [default: no]`

  This specifies whether information for (conditional) jumps should be collected. As above, callgrind_annotate currently is not able to show you the data. You have to use KCachegrind to get jump arrows in the annotated code.

7.4.5 Cost entity separation options

These options specify how event counts should be attributed to execution contexts. For example, they specify whether the recursion level or the call chain leading to a function should be taken into account, and whether the thread ID should be considered. Also see Section 7.3.3 [Avoiding cycles], page 83.

- `--separate-threads=<no|yes> [default: no]`

  This option specifies whether profile data should be generated separately for every thread. If yes, the file names get `-threadID` appended.

- `--separate-recs=<level> [default: 2]`

  Separate function recursions by at most <level> levels. See Section 7.3.3 [Avoiding cycles], page 83.

- `--separate-callers=<callers> [default: 0]`

  Separate contexts by at most <callers> functions in the call chain. See Section 7.3.3 [Avoiding cycles], page 83.

- `--skip-plt=<no|yes> [default: yes]`

  Ignore calls to/from PLT sections.

- `--fn-skip=<function>`

  Ignore calls to/from a given function. E.g. if you have a call chain A > B
  > C, and you specify function B to be ignored, you will only see A > C.

  This is very convenient to skip functions handling callback behaviour. For
  example, with the signal/slot mechanism in the Qt graphics library, you
  only want to see the function emitting a signal to call the slots connected
  to that signal. First, determine the real call chain to see the functions
  needed to be skipped, then use this option.

- `--fn-group<number>=<function>` Put a function into a separate group.
  This influences the context name for cycle avoidance. All functions inside
  such a group are treated as being the same for context name building,
  which resembles the call chain leading to a context. By specifying function
  groups with this option, you can shorten the context name, as functions
  in the same group will not appear in sequence in the name.

- `--separate-recs<number>=<function>`

  Separate <number> recursions for <function>. See Section 7.3.3 [Avoiding
  cycles], page 83.

- `--separate-callers<number>=<function>`

  Separate <number> callers for <function>. See Section 7.3.3 [Avoiding
  cycles], page 83.

7.4.6 Cache simulation options

- `--simulate-cache=<yes|no>` [default: no]

  Specify if you want to do full cache simulation. By default, only instruction
  read accesses will be profiled.

- `--simulate-hwpref=<yes|no>` [default: no]

  Specify whether simulation of a hardware prefetcher should be added which
  is able to detect stream access in the second level cache by comparing
  accesses to separate to each page. As the simulation can not decide about
  any timing issues of prefetching, it is assumed that any hardware prefetch
  triggered succeeds before a real access is done. Thus, this gives a best-case
  scenario by covering all possible stream accesses.

8 Massif: a heap profiler

To use this tool, you must specify `--tool=massif` on the Valgrind command line.[1]

8.1 Heap profiling

Massif is a heap profiler. It measures how much heap memory your program uses. This includes both the useful space, and the extra bytes allocated for book-keeping purposes and alignment purposes. It can also measure the size of your program's stack(s), although it does not do so by default.

Heap profiling can help you reduce the amount of memory your program uses. On modern machines with virtual memory, this provides the following benefits:

- It can speed up your program—a smaller program will interact better with your machine's caches and avoid paging.

- If your program uses lots of memory, it will reduce the chance that it exhausts your machine's swap space.

Also, there are certain space leaks that aren't detected by traditional leak-checkers, such as Memcheck's. That's because the memory isn't ever actually lost—a pointer remains to it—but it's not in use. Programs that have leaks like this can unnecessarily increase the amount of memory they are using over time. Massif can help identify these leaks.

Importantly, Massif tells you not only how much heap memory your program is using, it also gives very detailed information that indicates which parts of your program are responsible for allocating the heap memory.

8.2 Using Massif

First off, as for the other Valgrind tools, you should compile with debugging info (the -g flag). It shouldn't matter much what optimisation level you compile your program with, as this is unlikely to affect the heap memory usage.

Then, to gather heap profiling information about the program `prog`, type:

```
$ valgrind --tool=massif prog
```

The program will execute (slowly). Upon completion, no summary statistics are printed to Valgrind's commentary; all of Massif's profiling data is written to a file. By default, this file is called 'massif.out.<pid>', where '<pid>' is the process ID.

To see the information gathered by Massif in an easy-to-read form, use the ms_print script. If the output file's name is 'massif.out.12345', type:

---

[1] Please note that this documentation describes Massif version 3.3.0 and later. Massif was significantly overhauled for 3.3.0; versions 3.2.3 and earlier presented the profiling information an a quite different manner, and so this documentation only pertains to the later versions.

```
% ms_print massif.out.12345
```
ms_print will produce (a) a graph showing the memory consumption over the
program's execution, and (b) detailed information about the responsible allocation sites at various points in the program, including the point of peak memory
allocation. The use of a separate script for presenting the results is deliber-
ate: it separates the data gathering from its presentation, and means that new
methods of presenting the data can be added in the future.

8.2.1 An Example Program

An example will make things clear. Consider the following C program (annotated with line numbers) which allocates a number of different blocks on the
heap.

```
 1      #include <stdlib.h>
 2
 3      void g(void)
 4      {
 5          malloc(4000);
 6      }
 7
 8      void f(void)
 9      {
10          malloc(2000);
11          g();
12      }
13
14      int main(void)
15      {
16          int i;
17          int* a[10];
18
19          for (i = 0; i < 10; i++) {
20              a[i] = malloc(1000);
21          }
22
23          f();
24
25          g();
26
27          for (i = 0; i < 10; i++) {
28              free(a[i]);
29          }
30
31          return 0;
32      }
```

8.2.2 The Output Preamble

After running this program under Massif, the first part of ms_print's output contains a preamble which just states how the program, Massif and ms_print were each invoked:

```
--------------------------------------------------------
Command:             example
Massif arguments:    (none)
ms_print arguments:  massif.out.12797
--------------------------------------------------------
```

8.2.3 The Output Graph

The next part is the graph that shows how memory consumption occurred as the program executed:

```
Number of snapshots: 25
Detailed snapshots: [9, 14 (peak), 24]
```

Why is most of the graph empty, with only a couple of bars at the very end? By default, Massif uses "instructions executed" as the unit of time. For very short-run programs such as the example, most of the executed instructions involve the loading and dynamic linking of the program. The execution of main (and thus the heap allocations) only occur at the very end. For a short-running program like this, we can use the --time-unit=B option to specify that we want the time unit to instead be the number of bytes allocated/deallocated on the heap and stack(s).

If we re-run the program under Massif with this option, and then re-run ms_print, we get this more useful graph:

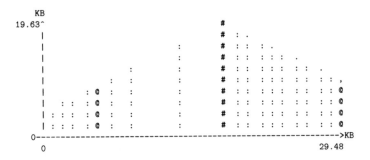

```
    KB
19.63^                              #
    |                               # : .
    |                           :   # : :  : .
    |                           :   # : :  : : :    .
    |                 :         :   # : :  : : :  : : .
    |                 :    :    :   # : :  : : :  : : : : ,
    |            : @   :    :    :   # : :  : : :  : : : : @
    |     : :    : @   :    :    :   # : :  : : :  : : : : @
    |   : : : :  : @   :    :    :   # : :  : : :  : : : : @
    |   : : : :  : @   :    :        #  : :  : : :  : : : : @
  0-+---------------------------------------------------------->KB
    0                                                      29.48

Number of snapshots: 25
Detailed snapshots: [9, 14 (peak), 24]
```

Each vertical bar represents a snapshot, i.e. a measurement of the memory usage at a certain point in time. The text at the bottom show that 25 snapshots were taken for this program, which is one per heap allocation/deallocation, plus a couple of extras. Massif starts by taking snapshots for every heap allocation/deallocation, but as a program runs for longer, it takes snapshots less frequently. It also discards older snapshots as the program goes on; when it reaches the maximum number of snapshots (100 by default, although changeable with the --max-snapshots option) half of them are deleted. This means that a reasonable number of snapshots are always maintained.

Most snapshots are *normal*, and only basic information is recorded for them. Normal snapshots are represented in the graph by bars consisting of : and . characters.

Some snapshots are *detailed*. Information about where allocations happened are recorded for these snapshots, as we will see shortly. Detailed snapshots are represented in the graph by bars consisting of @ and , characters. The text at the bottom show that 3 detailed snapshots were taken for this program (snapshots 9, 14 and 24). By default, every 10th snapshot is detailed, although this can be changed via the --detailed-freq option.

Finally, there is at most one *peak* snapshot. The peak snapshot is a detailed snapshot, and records the point where memory consumption was greatest. The peak snapshot is represented in the graph by a bar consisting of # and , characters. The text at the bottom shows that snapshot 14 was the peak. Note that for tiny programs that never deallocate heap memory, Massif will not record a peak snapshot.

Some more details about the peak: the peak is determined by looking at every allocation, i.e. it is *not* just the peak among the regular snapshots. However, recording the true peak is expensive, and so by default Massif records a peak whose size is within 1% of the size of the true peak. See the description of the --peak-inaccuracy option below for more details.

The following graph is from an execution of Konqueror, the KDE web browser. It shows what graphs for larger programs look like.

```
  MB
3.952^                                                          #.
     |                                                 ,  .. :@@#:
     |                                                ,@ :: :@@#::
     |                                           .@ :@@@ :: :@@#::
     |                                          ,: :@ :@@@ :: :@@#::
     |                                      @@:@: :@ :@@@ :: :@@#:::
     |                  .:@@:    .: ::: ::: @ :::@@:@: :@ :@@@ :: :@@#:::
     |            @: ::@@:   ::: :::::::: @ :::@@:@: :@ :@@@ :: :@@#::.
     |        , @: ::@@::  ::: :::::::: @ :::@@:@: :@ :@@@ :: :@@#:::
     |, :::::@ @: ::@@::  ::: :::::::: @ :::@@:@: :@ :@@@ :: :@@#:::
   0-+------------------------------------------------------------------>Mi
     0                                                            626.4
```

Number of snapshots: 63
Detailed snapshots: [3, 4, 10, 11, 15, 16, 29, 33, 34, 36, 39, 41,
                     42, 43, 44, 49, 50, 51, 53, 55, 56, 57 (peak)]

Note that the larger size units are KB, MB, GB, etc. As is typical for memory measurements, these are based on a multiplier of 1024, rather than the standard SI multiplier of 1,000. Strictly speaking, they should be written KiB, MiB, GiB, etc.

8.2.4 The Snapshot Details

Returning to our example, the graph is followed by the detailed information for each snapshot. The first nine snapshots are normal, so only a small amount of information is recorded for each one:

n	time (B)	total (B)	useful-heap (B)	extra-heap (B)	stacks (B)
0	0	0	0	0	0
1	1,008	1,008	1,000	8	0
2	2,016	2,016	2,000	16	0
3	3,024	3,024	3,000	24	0
4	4,032	4,032	4,000	32	0
5	5,040	5,040	5,000	40	0
6	6,048	6,048	6,000	48	0
7	7,056	7,056	7,000	56	0
8	8,064	8,064	8,000	64	0

Each normal snapshot records several things.

- Its number.

- The time it was taken. In this case, the time unit is bytes, due to the use of --time-unit=B.

- The total memory consumption at that point.

- The number of useful heap bytes allocated at that point. This reflects the number of bytes asked for by the program.

- The number of extra heap bytes allocated at that point. This reflects the number of bytes allocated in excess of what the program asked for. There are two sources of extra heap bytes.

  First, every heap block has administrative bytes associated with it. The exact number of administrative bytes depends on the details of the allocator. By default Massif assumes 8 bytes per block, as can be seen from the example, but this number can be changed via the --heap-admin option.

  Second, allocators often round up the number of bytes asked for to a larger number. By default, if N bytes are asked for, Massif rounds N up to the nearest multiple of 8 that is equal to or greater than N. This is typical behaviour for allocators, and is required to ensure that elements within the block are suitably aligned. The rounding size can be changed with the --alignment option, although it cannot be less than 8, and must be a power of two.

- The size of the stack(s). By default, stack profiling is off as it slows Massif down greatly. Therefore, the stack column is zero in the example.

The next snapshot is detailed. As well as the basic counts, it gives an allocation tree which indicates exactly which pieces of code were responsible for allocating heap memory:

```
9      9,072       9,072       9,000        72        0
99.21% (9,000B) (heap allocation functions)
    malloc/new/new[], --alloc-fns, etc.
->99.21% (9,000B) 0x804841A: main (example.c:20)
```

The allocation tree can be read from the top down. The first line indicates all heap allocation functions such as malloc and C++ new. All heap allocations go through these functions, and so all 9,000 useful bytes (which is 99.21% of all allocated bytes) go through them. But how were malloc and new called? At this point, every allocation so far has been due to line 21 inside main, hence the second line in the tree. The -> indicates that main (line 20) called malloc.

Let's see what the subsequent output shows happened next:

```
---------------------------------------------------------
 n     time    total  useful-heap  extra-heap  stacks
        (B)      (B)          (B)         (B)     (B)
---------------------------------------------------------
10   10,080   10,080       10,000          80       0
11   12,088   12,088       12,000          88       0
12   16,096   16,096       16,000          96       0
13   20,104   20,104       20,000         104       0
14   20,104   20,104       20,000         104       0
99.48% (20,000B) (heap allocation functions)
    malloc/new/new[], --alloc-fns, etc.
->49.74% (10,000B) 0x804841A: main (example.c:20)
|
->39.79% (8,000B) 0x80483C2: g (example.c:5)
| ->19.90% (4,000B) 0x80483E2: f (example.c:11)
| | ->19.90% (4,000B) 0x8048431: main (example.c:23)
```

```
| |
| ->19.90% (4,000B) 0x8048436: main (example.c:25)
|
->09.95% (2,000B) 0x80483DA: f (example.c:10)
   ->09.95% (2,000B) 0x8048431: main (example.c:23)
```

The first four snapshots are similar to the previous ones. But then the global allocation peak is reached, and a detailed snapshot is taken. Its allocation tree shows that 20,000B of useful heap memory has been allocated, and the lines and arrows indicate that this is from three different code locations: line 20, which is responsible for 10,000B (49.74%); line 5, which is responsible for 8,000B (39.79%); and line 10, which is responsible for 2,000B (9.95%).

We can then drill down further in the allocation tree. For example, of the 8,000B asked for by line 5, half of it was due to a call from line 11, and half was due to a call from line 25.

In short, Massif collates the stack trace of every single allocation point in the program into a single tree, which gives a complete picture of how and why all heap memory was allocated.

Note that the tree entries correspond not to functions, but to individual code locations. For example, if function A calls malloc, and function B calls A twice, once on line 10 and once on line 11, then the two calls will result in two distinct stack traces in the tree. In contrast, if B calls A repeatedly from line 15 (e.g. due to a loop), then each of those calls will be represented by the same stack trace in the tree.

Note also that tree entry with children in the example satisfies an invariant: the entry's size is equal to the sum of its children's sizes. For example, the first entry has size 20,000B, and its children have sizes 10,000B, 8,000B, and 2,000B. In general, this invariant almost always holds. However, in rare circumstances stack traces can be malformed, in which case a stack trace can be a sub-trace of another stack trace. This means that some entries in the tree may not satisfy the invariant—the entry's size will be greater than the sum of its children's sizes. Massif can sometimes detect when this happens; if it does, it issues a warning:

```
Warning: Malformed stack trace detected.
         In Massif's output, the size of an entry's child
         entries may not sum up to the entry's size as
         they normally do.
```

However, Massif does not detect and warn about every such occurrence. Fortunately, malformed stack traces are rare in practice.

Returning now to ms_print's output, the final part is similar:

n	time (B)	total (B)	useful-heap (B)	extra-heap (B)	stacks (B)
15	21,112	19,096	19,000	96	0
16	22,120	18,088	18,000	88	0
17	23,128	17,080	17,000	80	0
18	24,136	16,072	16,000	72	0

19	25,144	15,064	15,000	64	0
20	26,152	14,056	14,000	56	0
21	27,160	13,048	13,000	48	0
22	28,168	12,040	12,000	40	0
23	29,176	11,032	11,000	32	0
24	30,184	10,024	10,000	24	0

```
99.76% (10,000B) (heap allocation functions)
    malloc/new/new[], --alloc-fns, etc.
->79.81% (8,000B) 0x80483C2: g (example.c:5)
| ->39.90% (4,000B) 0x80483E2: f (example.c:11)
| | ->39.90% (4,000B) 0x8048431: main (example.c:23)
| |
| ->39.90% (4,000B) 0x8048436: main (example.c:25)
|
->19.95% (2,000B) 0x80483DA: f (example.c:10)
| ->19.95% (2,000B) 0x8048431: main (example.c:23)
|
->00.00% (0B) in 1+ places, all below ms_print's
threshold (01.00%)
```

The final detailed snapshot shows how the heap looked at termination. The 00.00% entry represents the code locations for which memory was allocated and then freed (line 20 in this case, the memory for which was freed on line 28). However, no code location details are given for this entry; by default, Massif only records the details for code locations responsible for more than 1% of useful memory bytes, and ms_print likewise only prints the details for code locations responsible for more than 1%. The entries that do not meet this threshold are aggregated. This avoids filling up the output with large numbers of unimportant entries. The thresholds threshold can be changed with the --threshold option that both Massif and ms_print support.

8.3 Massif Options

Massif-specific options are:

- --heap=<yes|no> [default: yes]

  Specifies whether heap profiling should be done.

- --heap-admin=<number> [default: 8]

  If heap profiling is enabled, gives the number of administrative bytes per block to use. This should be an estimate of the average, since it may vary. For example, the allocator used by glibc requires somewhere between 4 to 15 bytes per block, depending on various factors. It also requires admin space for freed blocks, although Massif does not account for this.

- --stacks=<yes|no> [default: yes]

  Specifies whether stack profiling should be done. This option slows Massif down greatly, and so is off by default. Note that Massif assumes that the main stack has size zero at start-up. This is not true, but measuring the actual stack size is not easy, and it reflects the size of the part of the main stack that a user program actually has control over.

- `--depth=<number>` `[default: 30]`

  Maximum depth of the allocation trees recorded for detailed snapshots. Increasing it will make Massif run somewhat more slowly, use more memory, and produce bigger output files.

- `--alloc-fn=<name>`

  Functions specified with this option will be treated as though they were a heap allocation function such as `malloc`. This is useful for functions that are wrappers to `malloc` or `new`, which can fill up the allocation trees with uninteresting information. This option can be specified multiple times on the command line, to name multiple functions.

  Note that overloaded C++ names must be written in full. Single quotes may be necessary to prevent the shell from breaking them up. For example:

  ```
  --alloc-fn='operator new(unsigned, std::nothrow_t
    const&amp;)'
  ```

  The full list of functions and operators that are by default considered allocation functions is as follows.

  ```
  malloc
  calloc
  realloc
  memalign
  __builtin_new
  __builtin_vec_new
  operator new(unsigned)
  operator new(unsigned long)
  operator new[](unsigned)
  operator new[](unsigned long)
  operator new(unsigned, std::nothrow_t const&)
  operator new[](unsigned, std::nothrow_t const&)
  operator new(unsigned long, std::nothrow_t const&)
  operator new[](unsigned long, std::nothrow_t const&)
  ```

- `--threshold=<m.n>` `[default: 1.0]`

  The significance threshold for heap allocations, as a percentage. Allocation tree entries that account for less than this will be aggregated. Note that this should be specified in tandem with ms_print's option of the same name.

- `--peak-inaccuracy=<m.n>` `[default: 1.0]`

  Massif does not necessarily record the actual global memory allocation peak; by default it records a peak only when the global memory allocation size exceeds the previous peak by at least 1.0%. This is because there can be many local allocation peaks along the way, and doing a detailed snapshot for every one would be expensive and wasteful, as all but one of them will be later discarded. This inaccuracy can be changed (even to 0.0%) via this option, but Massif will run drastically slower as the number approaches zero.

- `--time-unit=i|ms|B [default: i]`

  The time unit used for the profiling. There are three possibilities: instructions executed (i), which is good for most cases; real (wallclock) time (ms, i.e. milliseconds), which is sometimes useful; and bytes allocated/deallocated on the heap and/or stack (B), which is useful for very short-run programs, and for testing purposes, because it is the most reproducible across different machines.

- `--detailed-freq=<n> [default: 10]`

  Frequency of detailed snapshots. With --detailed-freq=1, every snapshot is detailed.

- `--max-snapshots=<n> [default: 100]`

  The maximum number of snapshots recorded. If set to N, for all programs except very short-running ones, the final number of snapshots will be between N/2 and N.

- `--massif-out-file=<file> [default: massif.out.%p]`

  Write the profile data to file rather than to the default output file, massif.out.<pid>. The %p and %q format specifiers can be used to embed the process ID and/or the contents of an environment variable in the name, as is the case for the core option --log-file. See Section 3.6.2 [Basic Options], page 18 for details.

- `--alignment=<n> [default: 1.0]`

  The minimum alignment (and thus size) of heap blocks.

8.4 ms_print Options

ms_print's options are:

- `-h, --help`

  `-v, --version`

  Help and version, as usual.

- `--threshold=<m.n> [default: 1.0]`

  Same as Massif's --threshold, but applied after profiling rather than during.

- `--x=<m.n> [default: 72]`

  Width of the graph, in columns.

- `--y=<n> [default: 20]`

  Height of the graph, in rows.

8.5 Massif's output file format

Massif's file format is plain text (i.e. not binary) and deliberately easy to read for both humans and machines. Nonetheless, the exact format is not described here. This is because the format is currently very Massif-specific. We plan to make the format more general, and thus suitable for possible use with other tools. Once this has been done, the format will be documented here.

9 Helgrind: a thread error detector

To use this tool, you must specify `--tool=helgrind` on the Valgrind command line.

9.1 Overview

Helgrind is a Valgrind tool for detecting synchronisation errors in C, C++ and Fortran programs that use the POSIX pthreads threading primitives.

The main abstractions in POSIX pthreads are: a set of threads sharing a common address space, thread creation, thread joinage, thread exit, mutexes (locks), condition variables (inter-thread event notifications), reader-writer locks, and semaphores.

Helgrind is aware of all these abstractions and tracks their effects as accurately as it can. Currently it does not correctly handle pthread barriers and pthread spinlocks, although it will not object if you use them. On x86 and amd64 platforms, it understands and partially handles implicit locking arising from the use of the LOCK instruction prefix.

Helgrind can detect three classes of errors, which are discussed in detail in the next three sections:

1. Misuses of the POSIX pthreads API. (see Section 9.2 [API Checks], page 100)

2. Potential deadlocks arising from lock ordering problems. (see Section 9.3 [Lock Orders], page 101)

3. Data races—accessing memory without adequate locking. (see Section 9.4 [Data Races], page 102)

Following those is a section containing hints and tips on how to get the best out of Helgrind. (see Section 9.5 [Helgrind Effective Use], page 111)

Then there is a summary of command-line options. (see Section 9.6 [Helgrind Options], page 115)

Finally, there is a brief summary of areas in which Helgrind could be improved. (see Section 9.7 [To Do List], page 116)

9.2 Detected errors: Misuses of the POSIX pthreads API

Helgrind intercepts calls to many POSIX pthreads functions, and is therefore able to report on various common problems. Although these are unglamourous errors, their presence can lead to undefined program behaviour and hard-to-find bugs later in execution. The detected errors are:

- unlocking an invalid mutex
- unlocking a not-locked mutex
- unlocking a mutex held by a different thread
- destroying an invalid or a locked mutex
- recursively locking a non-recursive mutex
- deallocation of memory that contains a locked mutex
- passing mutex arguments to functions expecting reader-writer lock arguments, and vice versa
- when a POSIX pthread function fails with an error code that must be handled
- when a thread exits whilst still holding locked locks
- calling pthread_cond_wait with a not-locked mutex, or one locked by a different thread

Checks pertaining to the validity of mutexes are generally also performed for reader-writer locks.

Various kinds of this-can't-possibly-happen events are also reported. These usually indicate bugs in the system threading library.

Reported errors always contain a primary stack trace indicating where the error was detected. They may also contain auxiliary stack traces giving additional information. In particular, most errors relating to mutexes will also tell you where that mutex first came to Helgrind's attention (the was first observed at part), so you have a chance of figuring out which mutex it is referring to. For example:

```
Thread #1 unlocked a not-locked lock at 0x7FEFFFA90
    at 0x4C2408D: pthread_mutex_unlock (hg_intercepts.c:492)
    by 0x40073A: nearly_main (tc09_bad_unlock.c:27)
    by 0x40079B: main (tc09_bad_unlock.c:50)
  Lock at 0x7FEFFFA90 was first observed
    at 0x4C25D01: pthread_mutex_init (hg_intercepts.c:326)
    by 0x40071F: nearly_main (tc09_bad_unlock.c:23)
    by 0x40079B: main (tc09_bad_unlock.c:50)
```

Helgrind has a way of summarising thread identities, as evidenced here by the text Thread #1. This is so that it can speak about threads and sets of threads without overwhelming you with details. See below (see Section 9.4.6 [Race Error Messages], page 109) for more information on interpreting error messages.

9.3 Detected errors: Inconsistent Lock Orderings

In this section, and in general, to "acquire" a lock simply means to lock that lock, and to "release" a lock means to unlock it.

Helgrind monitors the order in which threads acquire locks. This allows it to detect potential deadlocks which could arise from the formation of cycles of locks. Detecting such inconsistencies is useful because, whilst actual deadlocks are fairly obvious, potential deadlocks may never be discovered during testing and could later lead to hard-to-diagnose in-service failures.

The simplest example of such a problem is as follows.

• Imagine some shared resource R, which, for whatever reason, is guarded by two locks, L1 and L2, which must both be held when R is accessed.

• Suppose a thread acquires L1, then L2, and proceeds to access R. The implication of this is that all threads in the program must acquire the two locks in the order first L1 then L2. Not doing so risks deadlock.

• The deadlock could happen if two threads—call them T1 and T2—both want to access R. Suppose T1 acquires L1 first, and T2 acquires L2 first. Then T1 tries to acquire L2, and T2 tries to acquire L1, but those locks are both already held. So T1 and T2 become deadlocked.

Helgrind builds a directed graph indicating the order in which locks have been acquired in the past. When a thread acquires a new lock, the graph is updated, and then checked to see if it now contains a cycle. The presence of a cycle indicates a potential deadlock involving the locks in the cycle.

In simple situations, where the cycle only contains two locks, Helgrind will show where the required order was established:

```
Thread #1:
  lock order "0x7FEFFFAB0 before 0x7FEFFFA80" violated
    at 0x4C23C91: pthread_mutex_lock (hg_intercepts.c:388)
    by 0x40081F: main (tc13_laog1.c:24)
  Required order was established by acquisition of lock
  at 0x7FEFFFAB0
    at 0x4C23C91: pthread_mutex_lock (hg_intercepts.c:388)
    by 0x400748: main (tc13_laog1.c:17)
  followed by a later acquisition of lock at 0x7FEFFFA80
    at 0x4C23C91: pthread_mutex_lock (hg_intercepts.c:388)
    by 0x400773: main (tc13_laog1.c:18)
```

When there are more than two locks in the cycle, the error is equally serious. However, at present Helgrind does not show the locks involved, so as to avoid flooding you with information. That could be fixed in future. For example, here is a an example involving a cycle of five locks from a naive implementation the famous Dining Philosophers problem (see helgrind/tests/tc14_laog_dinphils.c). In this case Helgrind has detected that all 5 philosophers could simultaneously pick up their left fork and then deadlock whilst waiting to pick up their right forks.

```
Thread #6: lock order "0x6010C0 before 0x601160" violated
   at 0x4C23C91: pthread_mutex_lock (hg_intercepts.c:388)
   by 0x4007C0: dine (tc14_laog_dinphils.c:19)
   by 0x4C25DF7: mythread_wrapper (hg_intercepts.c:178)
   by 0x4E2F09D: start_thread
   (in /lib64/libpthread-2.5.so)
   by 0x51054CC: clone (in /lib64/libc-2.5.so)
```

9.4 Detected errors: Data Races

A data race happens, or could happen, when two threads access a shared memory location without using suitable locks to ensure single-threaded access. Such missing locking can cause obscure timing dependent bugs. Ensuring programs are race-free is one of the central difficulties of threaded programming.

Reliably detecting races is a difficult problem, and most of Helgrind's internals are devoted to do dealing with it. As a consequence this section is somewhat long and involved. We begin with a simple example.

9.4.1 A Simple Data Race

About the simplest possible example of a race is as follows. In this program, it is impossible to know what the value of var is at the end of the program. Is it 2 ? Or 1 ?

```
#include <pthread.h>

int var = 0;

void* child_fn ( void* arg ) {
   var++; /* Unprotected relative to parent : line 6 */
   return NULL;
}

int main ( void ) {
   pthread_t child;
   pthread_create(&child, NULL, child_fn, NULL);
   var++; /* Unprotected relative to child : line 13 */
   pthread_join(child, NULL);
   return 0;
}
```

The problem is there is nothing to stop var being updated simultaneously by both threads. A correct program would protect var with a lock of type pthread_mutex_t, which is acquired before each access and released afterwards. Helgrind's output for this program is:

```
Thread #1 is the program's root thread

Thread #2 was created
   at 0x510548E: clone (in /lib64/libc-2.5.so)
   by 0x4E2F305: do_clone (in /lib64/libpthread-2.5.so)
   by 0x4E2F7C5: pthread_create@@GLIBC_2.2.5
```

```
    (in /lib64/libpthread-2.5.so)
    by 0x4C23870: pthread_create@* (hg_intercepts.c:198)
    by 0x4005F1: main (simple_race.c:12)

  Possible data race during write of size 4 at 0x601034
    at 0x4005F2: main (simple_race.c:13)
  Old state: shared-readonly by threads #1, #2
  New state: shared-modified by threads #1, #2
  Reason:    this thread, #1, holds no consistent locks
  Location 0x601034 has never been protected by any lock
```

This is quite a lot of detail for an apparently simple error. The last clause is the main error message. It says there is a race as a result of a write of size 4 (bytes), at 0x601034, which is presumably the address of var, happening in function main at line 13 in the program.

Note that it is purely by chance that the race is reported for the parent thread's access. It could equally have been reported instead for the child's access, at line 6. The error will only be reported for one of the locations, since neither the parent nor child is, by itself, incorrect. It is only when both access var without a lock that an error exists.

The error message shows some other interesting details. The sections below explain them. Here we merely note their presence:

- Helgrind maintains some kind of state machine for the memory location in question, hence the Old state: and New state: lines.

- Helgrind keeps track of which threads have accessed the location: threads #1, #2. Before printing the main error message, it prints the creation points of these two threads, so you can see which threads it is referring to.

- Helgrind tries to provide an explanation of why the race exists: Location 0x601034 has never been protected by any lock.

Understanding the memory state machine is central to understanding Helgrind's race-detection algorithm. The next three subsections explain this.

9.4.2 Helgrind's Memory State Machine

Helgrind tracks the state of every byte of memory used by your program. There are a number of states, but only three are interesting:

- Exclusive: memory in this state is regarded as owned exclusively by one particular thread. That thread may read and write it without a lock. Even in highly threaded programs, the majority of locations never leave the Exclusive state, since most data is thread-private.

- Shared-Readonly: memory in this state is regarded as shared by multiple threads. In this state, any thread may read the memory without a lock, reflecting the fact that readonly data may safely be shared between threads without locking.

- Shared-Modified: memory in this state is regarded as shared by multiple threads, at least one of which has written to it. All participating threads must hold at least one lock in common when accessing the memory. If no such lock exists, Helgrind reports a race error.

Let's review the simple example above with this in mind. When the program starts, var is not in any of these states. Either the parent or child thread gets to its var++ first, and thereby thereby gets Exclusive ownership of the location.

The later-running thread now arrives at its var++ statement. It first reads the existing value from memory. Because var is currently marked as owned exclusively by the other thread, its state is changed to shared-readonly by both threads.

This same thread adds one to the value it has and stores it back in var. This causes another state change, this time to the shared-modified state. Because Helgrind has also been tracking which threads hold which locks, it can see that var is in shared-modified state but no lock has been used to consistently protect it. Hence a race is reported exactly at the transition from shared-readonly to shared-modified.

The essence of the algorithm is this. Helgrind keeps track of each memory location that has been accessed by more than one thread. For each such location it incrementally infers the set of locks which have consistently been used to protect that location. If the location's lockset becomes empty, and at some point one of the threads attempts to write to it, a race is then reported.

This technique is known as "lockset inference" and was introduced in: *"Eraser: A Dynamic Data Race Detector for Multithreaded Programs"*, (Stefan Savage, Michael Burrows, Greg Nelson, Patrick Sobalvarro and Thomas Anderson, *ACM Transactions on Computer Systems*, 15(4):391-411, November 1997).

Lockset inference has since been widely implemented, studied and extended. Helgrind incorporates several refinements aimed at avoiding the high false error rate that naive versions of the algorithm suffer from. A summary of the complete algorithm used by Helgrind (see Section 9.4.5 [Race Det Summary], page 107) is presented below. First, however, it is important to understand details of transitions pertaining to the Exclusive-ownership state.

9.4.3 Transfers of Exclusive Ownership Between Threads

As presented, the algorithm is far too strict. It reports many errors in perfectly correct, widely used parallel programming constructions, for example, using child worker threads and worker thread pools.

To avoid these false errors, we must refine the algorithm so that it keeps memory in an Exclusive ownership state in cases where it would otherwise decay into a shared-readonly or shared-modified state. Recall that Exclusive ownership is special in that it grants the owning thread the right to access memory without use of any locks. In order to support worker-thread and worker-thread-pool idioms, we will allow threads to steal exclusive ownership of memory from other threads under certain circumstances.

Here's an example. Imagine a parent thread creates child threads to do units of work. For each unit of work, the parent allocates a work buffer, fills it in, and creates the child thread, handing it a pointer to the buffer. The child reads/writes the buffer and eventually exits, and the waiting parent then extracts the results from the buffer:

```
typedef ... Buffer;

pthread_t child;
Buffer    buf;

/* ---- Parent ---- */              /* ---- Child ---- */

/* parent writes workload into buf */
pthread_create( &child, child_fn, &buf );

/* parent does not read */          void child_fn (Buffer* buf) {
/* or write buf */                  /* read/write buf */
                                    }

pthread_join ( child );
/* parent reads results from buf */
```

Although buf is accessed by both threads, neither uses locks, yet the program is race-free. The essential observation is that the child's creation and exit create synchronisation events between it and the parent. These force the child's accesses to buf to happen after the parent initialises buf, and before the parent reads the results from buf.

To model this, Helgrind allows the child to steal, from the parent, exclusive ownership of any memory exclusively owned by the parent before the pthread_create call. Similarly, once the parent's pthread_join call returns, it can steal back ownership of memory exclusively owned by the child. In this way ownership of buf is transferred from parent to child and back, so the basic algorithm does not report any races despite the absence of any locking.

Note that the child may only steal memory owned by the parent prior to the pthread_create call. If the child attempts to read or write memory which is also accessed by the parent in between the pthread_create and pthread_join calls, an error is still reported.

This technique was introduced with the name "thread lifetime segments" in *"Runtime Checking of Multithreaded Applications with Visual Threads"*, (Jerry J. Harrow, Jr, Proceedings of the 7th International SPIN Workshop on Model Checking of Software Stanford, California, USA, August 2000, LNCS 1885, pp331–342). Helgrind implements an extended version of it. Specifically, Helgrind allows transfer of exclusive ownership in the following situations:

- At thread creation: a child can acquire ownership of memory held exclusively by the parent prior to the child's creation.

- At thread joining: the joiner (thread not exiting) can acquire ownership of memory held exclusively by the joinee (thread that is exiting) at the point it exited.

- At condition variable signallings and broadcasts. A thread Tw which completes a pthread_cond_wait call as a result of a signal or broadcast on the same condition variable by some other thread Ts, may acquire ownership of memory held exclusively by Ts prior to the pthread_cond_signal/broadcast call.

- At semaphore posts (sem_post) calls. A thread Tw which completes a sem_wait call as a result of a sem_post call on the same semaphore by some other thread Tp, may acquire ownership of memory held exclusively by Tp prior to the sem_post call.

9.4.4 Restoration of Exclusive Ownership

Another common idiom is to partition the lifetime of the program as a whole into several distinct phases. In some of those phases, a memory location may be accessed by multiple threads and so require locking. In other phases only one thread exists and so can access the memory without locking. For example:

```
int           var = 0;  /* shared variable */
pthread_mutex_t mx
   = PTHREAD_MUTEX_INITIALIZER; /* guard for var */
pthread_t     child;

/* ---- Parent ---- */                  /* ---- Child ---- */

var += 1; /* no lock used */

pthread_create( &child,
child_fn, NULL );

                                        void child_fn (void* uu)
                                        {
pthread_mutex_lock(&mx);                   pthread_mutex_lock(&mx);
var += 2;                                  var += 3;
pthread_mutex_unlock(&mx);                 pthread_mutex_unlock(&mx);
                                        }

pthread_join ( child );

var += 4; /* no lock used */
```

This program is correct, but using only the mechanisms described so far, Helgrind would report an error at var += 4. This is because, by that point, var is marked as being in the state "shared-modified and protected by the lock mx", but is being accessed without locking. Really, what we want is for var to return to the parent thread's exclusive ownership after the child thread has exited.

To make this possible, for every memory location Helgrind also keeps track of all the threads that have accessed that location—its threadset. When a thread Tquitter joins back to Tstayer, Helgrind examines the locksets of all memory in shared-modified or shared-readable state. In each such lockset, if Tquitter is mentioned, it is removed and replaced by Tstayer. If, as a result, a lockset becomes a singleton set containing Tstayer, then the location's state is changed to belongs-exclusively-to-Tstayer.

In our example, the result is exactly as we desire: var is reacquired exclusively by the parent after the child exits.

More generally, when a group of threads merges back to a single thread via a cascade of pthread_join calls, any memory shared by the group (or a subset of it) ends up being owned exclusively by the sole surviving thread. This significantly enhances Helgrind's flexibility, since it means that each memory location may make arbitrarily many transitions between exclusive and shared ownership. Furthermore, a different lock may protect the location during each period of shared ownership.

9.4.5 A Summary of the Race Detection Algorithm

Helgrind looks for memory locations which are accessed by more than one thread. For each such location, Helgrind records which of the program's locks were held by the accessing thread at the time of each access. The hope is to discover that there is indeed at least one lock which is consistently used by all threads to protect that location. If no such lock can be found, then there is apparently no consistent locking strategy being applied for that location, and so a possible data race might result. Helgrind accordingly reports an error.

In practice this discipline is far too simplistic, and is unusable since it reports many races in some widely used and known-correct programming disciplines. Helgrind's checking therefore incorporates many refinements to this basic idea, and can be summarised as follows:

The following thread events are intercepted and monitored:

- thread creation and exiting
  - pthread_create
  - pthread_join
  - pthread_exit
- lock acquisition and release
  - pthread_mutex_lock
  - pthread_mutex_unlock
  - pthread_rwlock_rdlock
  - pthread_rwlock_wrlock
  - pthread_rwlock_unlock
- inter-thread event notifications
  - pthread_cond_wait
  - pthread_cond_signal
  - pthread_cond_broadcast
  - sem_wait
  - sem_post

Memory allocation and deallocation events are intercepted and monitored:

- malloc/new/free/delete and variants
- stack allocation and deallocation

All memory accesses are intercepted and monitored.

By observing the above events, Helgrind can infer certain aspects of the program's locking discipline. Programs which adhere to the following rules are considered to be acceptable:

- A thread may allocate memory, and write initial values into it, without locking. That thread is regarded as owning the memory exclusively.

- A thread may read and write memory which it owns exclusively, without locking.

- Memory which is owned exclusively by one thread may be read by that thread and others without locking. However, in this situation no thread may do unlocked writes to the memory (except for the owner thread's initializing write).

- Memory which is shared between multiple threads, one or more of which writes to it, must be protected by a lock which is correctly acquired and released by all threads accessing the memory.

Any violation of this discipline will cause an error to be reported. However, two exemptions apply:

- A thread Y can acquire exclusive ownership of memory previously owned exclusively by a different thread X providing X's last access and Y's first access are separated by one of the following synchronization events:

  - X creates thread Y
  - X joins back to Y
  - X uses a condition-variable to signal at Y, and Y is waiting for that event
  - Y completes a semaphore wait as a result of X signalling on that same semaphore

  This refinement allows Helgrind to correctly track the ownership state of inter-thread buffers used in the worker-thread and worker-thread-pool concurrent programming idioms (styles).

- Similarly, if thread Y joins back to thread X, memory exclusively owned by Y becomes exclusively owned by X instead. Also, memory that has been shared only by X and Y becomes exclusively owned by X. More generally, memory that has been shared by X, Y and some arbitrary other set S of threads is re-marked as shared by X and S. Hence, under the right circumstances, memory shared amongst multiple threads, all of which join into just one, can revert to the exclusive ownership state.

  In effect, each memory location may make arbitrarily many transitions between exclusive and shared ownership. Furthermore, a different lock may protect the location during each period of shared ownership. This significantly enhances the flexibility of the algorithm.

The ownership state, accessing thread-set and related lock-set for each memory location are tracked at 8-bit granularity. This means the algorithm is precise even for 16- and 8-bit memory accesses.

Helgrind correctly handles reader-writer locks in this framework. Locations shared between multiple threads can be protected during reads by locks held in either read-mode or write-mode, but can only be protected during writes by locks held in write-mode. Normal POSIX mutexes are treated as if they are reader-writer locks which are only ever held in write-mode.

Helgrind correctly handles POSIX mutexes for which recursive locking is allowed.

Helgrind partially correctly handles x86 and amd64 memory access instructions preceded by a LOCK prefix. Writes are correctly handled, by pretending that the LOCK prefix implies acquisition and release of a magic "bus hardware lock" mutex before and after the instruction. This unfortunately requires subsequent reads from such locations to also use a LOCK prefix, which is not required by the real hardware. Helgrind does not offer any equivalent handling for atomic sequences on PowerPC/POWER platforms created by the use of lwarx/stwcx instructions.

9.4.6 Interpreting Race Error Messages

Helgrind's race detection algorithm collects a lot of information, and tries to present it in a helpful way when a race is detected. Here's an example:

```
Thread #2 was created
   at 0x510548E: clone (in /lib64/libc-2.5.so)
   by 0x4E2F305: do_clone (in /lib64/libpthread-2.5.so)
   by 0x4E2F7C5: pthread_create@@GLIBC_2.2.5
   (in /lib64/libpthread-2.5.so)
   by 0x4C23870: pthread_create@* (hg_intercepts.c:198)
   by 0x400CEF: main (tc17_sembar.c:195)

// And the same for threads #3, #4 and #5

Possible data race during read of size 4 at 0x602174
   at 0x400BE5: gomp_barrier_wait (tc17_sembar.c:122)
   by 0x400C44: child (tc17_sembar.c:161)
   by 0x4C25DF7: mythread_wrapper (hg_intercepts.c:178)
   by 0x4E2F09D: start_thread
   (in /lib64/libpthread-2.5.so)
   by 0x51054CC: clone (in /lib64/libc-2.5.so)
Old state: shared-modified by threads #2, #3, #4, #5
New state: shared-modified by threads #2, #3, #4, #5
Reason:   this thread, #2, holds no consistent locks
Last consistently used lock for 0x602174
was first observed
   at 0x4C25D01: pthread_mutex_init (hg_intercepts.c:326)
   by 0x4009E4: gomp_barrier_init (tc17_sembar.c:46)
   by 0x400CBC: main (tc17_sembar.c:192)
```

Helgrind first announces the creation points of any threads referenced in the
error message. This is so it can speak concisely about threads and sets of threads
without repeatedly printing their creation point call stacks. Each thread is only
ever announced once, the first time it appears in any Helgrind error message.

The main error message begins at the text "Possible data race during
read". At the start is information you would expect to see—address and size
of the racing access, whether a read or a write, and the call stack at the point
it was detected.

More interesting is the state transition caused by this access. This memory is
already in the shared-modified state, and up to now has been consistently protected by at least one lock. However, the thread making the access in question
(thread #2, here) does not hold any locks in common with those held during
all previous accesses to the location—"no consistent locks", in other words.

Finally, Helgrind shows the lock which has protected this location in all previous accesses. (If there is more than one, only one is shown). This can be a
useful hint, because it typically shows the lock that the programmers intended
to use to protect the location, but in this case forgot.

Here are some more examples of race reports. This not an exhaustive list
of combinations, but should give you some insight into how to interpret the
output.

```
Possible data race during write ...
   Old state: shared-readonly by threads #1, #2, #3
   New state: shared-modified by threads #1, #2, #3
   Reason:    this thread, #3, holds no consistent locks
   Location ... has never been protected by any lock
```

The location is shared by 3 threads, all of which have been reading it without
locking ("has never been protected by any lock"). Now one of them is writing
it. Regardless of whether the writer has a lock or not, this is still an error,
because the write races against the previously observed reads.

```
Possible data race during read ...
   Old state: shared-modified by threads #1, #2, #3
   New state: shared-modified by threads #1, #2, #3
   Reason:    this thread, #3, holds no consistent locks
   Last consistently used lock for ...
   was first observed ...
```

The location is shared by 3 threads, all of which have been reading and
writing it while (as required) holding at least one lock in common. Now it is
being read without that lock being held. In the "Last consistently used lock"
part, Helgrind offers its best guess as to the identity of the lock that should
have been used.

```
Possible data race during write ...
   Old state: owned exclusively by thread #4
   New state: shared-modified by threads #4, #5
   Reason:    this thread, #5, holds no locks at all
```

A location that has so far been accessed exclusively by thread #4 has now
been written by thread #5, without use of any lock. This can be a sign that

the programmer did not consider the possibility of the location being shared between threads, or, alternatively, forgot to use the appropriate lock.

Note that thread #4 exclusively owns the location, and so has the right to access it without holding a lock. However, this message does not say that thread #4 is not using a lock for this location. Indeed, it could be using a lock for the location because it intends to make it available to other threads, one of which is thread #5—and thread #5 has forgotten to use the lock.

Also, this message implies that Helgrind did not see any synchronisation event between threads #4 and #5 that would have allowed #5 to acquire exclusive ownership from #4. See Section 9.4.3 [Excl Transfers], page 104 for a discussion of transfers of exclusive ownership states between threads.

9.5 Hints and Tips for Effective Use of Helgrind

Helgrind can be very helpful in finding and resolving threading-related problems. Like all sophisticated tools, it is most effective when you understand how to play to its strengths.

Helgrind will be less effective when you merely throw an existing threaded program at it and try to make sense of any reported errors. It will be more effective if you design threaded programs from the start in a way that helps Helgrind verify correctness. The same is true for finding memory errors with Memcheck, but applies more here, because thread checking is a harder problem. Consequently it is much easier to write a correct program for which Helgrind falsely reports (threading) errors than it is to write a correct program for which Memcheck falsely reports (memory) errors.

With that in mind, here are some tips, listed most important first, for getting reliable results and avoiding false errors. The first two are critical. Any violations of them will swamp you with huge numbers of false data-race errors.

1. Make sure your application, and all the libraries it uses, use the POSIX threading primitives. Helgrind needs to be able to see all events pertaining to thread creation, exit, locking and other synchronisation events. To do so it intercepts many POSIX pthread_ functions.

   Do not roll your own threading primitives (mutexes, etc) from combinations of the Linux futex syscall, counters and wotnot. These throw Helgrind's internal what's-going-on models way off course and will give bogus results.

   Also, do not reimplement existing POSIX abstractions using other POSIX abstractions. For example, don't build your own semaphore routines or reader-writer locks from POSIX mutexes and condition variables. Instead use POSIX reader-writer locks and semaphores directly, since Helgrind supports them directly.

   Helgrind directly supports the following POSIX threading abstractions: mutexes, reader-writer locks, condition variables (but see below), and semaphores. Currently spinlocks and barriers are not supported, although they could be in future. A prototype "safe" implementation of barriers, based on semaphores, is available: please contact the Valgrind authors for details.

At the time of writing, the following popular Linux packages are known to implement their own threading primitives:

- Qt version 4.X. Qt 3.X is fine, but not 4.X. Helgrind contains partial direct support for Qt 4.X threading, but this is not yet in a usable state. Assistance from folks knowledgeable in Qt 4 threading internals would be appreciated.

- Runtime support library for GNU OpenMP (part of GCC), at least GCC versions 4.2 and 4.3. With some minor effort of modifying the GNU OpenMP runtime support sources, it is possible to use Helgrind on GNU OpenMP compiled codes. Please contact the Valgrind authors for details.

2. Avoid memory recycling. If you can't avoid it, you must use tell Helgrind what is going on via the `VALGRIND_HG_CLEAN_MEMORY` client request (in `helgrind.h`).

Helgrind is aware of standard memory allocation and deallocation that occurs via malloc/free/new/delete and from entry and exit of stack frames. In particular, when memory is deallocated via free, delete, or function exit, Helgrind considers that memory clean, so when it is eventually reallocated, its history is irrelevant.

However, it is common practice to implement memory recycling schemes. In these, memory to be freed is not handed to malloc/delete, but instead put into a pool of free buffers to be handed out again as required. The problem is that Helgrind has no way to know that such memory is logically no longer in use, and its history is irrelevant. Hence you must make that explicit, using the `VALGRIND_HG_CLEAN_MEMORY` client request to specify the relevant address ranges. It's easiest to put these requests into the pool manager code, and use them either when memory is returned to the pool, or is allocated from it.

3. Avoid POSIX condition variables. If you can, use POSIX semaphores (sem_t, sem_post, sem_wait) to do inter-thread event signalling. Semaphores with an initial value of zero are particularly useful for this.

Helgrind only partially correctly handles POSIX condition variables. This is because Helgrind can see inter-thread dependencies between a pthread_cond_wait call and a pthread_cond_signal/broadcast call only if the waiting thread actually gets to the rendezvous first (so that it actually calls pthread_cond_wait). It can't see dependencies between the threads if the signaller arrives first. In the latter case, POSIX guidelines imply that the associated boolean condition still provides an inter-thread synchronisation event, but one which is invisible to Helgrind.

The result of Helgrind missing some inter-thread synchronisation events is to cause it to report false positives. That's because missing such events reduces the extent to which it can transfer exclusive memory ownership between threads. So memory may end up in a shared-modified state when that was not intended by the application programmers.

The root cause of this synchronisation lossage is particularly hard to understand, so an example is helpful. It was discussed at length by Arndt

Muehlenfeld (*Runtime Race Detection in Multi-Threaded Programs*, Dissertation, TU Graz, Austria). The canonical POSIX-recommended usage scheme for condition variables is as follows:

```
b    is a Boolean condition (False most of the time)
cv   is a condition variable
mx   is its associated mutex
```

```
Signaller:                    Waiter:

lock(mx)                      lock(mx)
b = True                      while (b == False)
signal(cv)                        wait(cv,mx)
unlock(mx)                    unlock(mx)
```

Assume b is False most of the time. If the waiter arrives at the rendezvous first, it enters its while-loop, waits for the signaller to signal, and eventually proceeds. Helgrind sees the signal, notes the dependency, and all is well.

If the signaller arrives first, b is set to true, and the signal disappears into nowhere. When the waiter later arrives, it does not enter its while-loop and simply carries on. But even in this case, the waiter code following the while-loop cannot execute until the signaller sets b to True. Hence there is still the same inter-thread dependency, but this time it is through an arbitrary in-memory condition, and Helgrind cannot see it.

By comparison, Helgrind's detection of inter-thread dependencies caused by semaphore operations is believed to be exactly correct.

As far as I know, a solution to this problem that does not require source-level annotation of condition-variable wait loops is beyond the current state of the art.

4. Make sure you are using a supported Linux distribution. At present, Helgrind only properly supports x86-linux and amd64-linux with glibc-2.3 or later. The latter restriction means we only support glibc's NPTL threading implementation. The old LinuxThreads implementation is not supported.

   Unsupported targets may work to varying degrees. In particular ppc32-linux and ppc64-linux running NTPL should work, but you will get false race errors because Helgrind does not know how to properly handle atomic instruction sequences created using the lwarx/stwcx instructions.

5. Round up all finished threads using pthread_join. Avoid detaching threads: don't create threads in the detached state, and don't call pthread_detach on existing threads.

   Using pthread_join to round up finished threads provides a clear synchronisation point that both Helgrind and programmers can see. This synchronisation point allows Helgrind to adjust its memory ownership models as described extensively above (see Section 9.4.3 [Excl Transfers], page 104), which helps Helgrind produce more accurate error reports.

   If you don't call pthread_join on a thread, Helgrind has no way to know when it finishes, relative to any significant synchronisation points for other threads in the program. So it assumes that the thread lingers indefinitely and can potentially interfere indefinitely with the memory state of the program. It has every right to assume that—after all, it might really be the case that, for scheduling reasons, the exiting thread did run very slowly in the last stages of its life.

6. Perform thread debugging (with Helgrind) and memory debugging (with Memcheck) together.

   Helgrind tracks the state of memory in detail, and memory management bugs in the application are liable to cause confusion. In extreme cases, applications which do many invalid reads and writes (particularly to freed memory) have been known to crash Helgrind. So, ideally, you should make your application Memcheck-clean before using Helgrind.

   It may be impossible to make your application Memcheck-clean unless you first remove threading bugs. In particular, it may be difficult to remove all reads and writes to freed memory in multithreaded C++ destructor sequences at program termination. So, ideally, you should make your application Helgrind-clean before using Memcheck.

   Since this circularity is obviously unresolvable, at least bear in mind that Memcheck and Helgrind are to some extent complementary, and you may need to use them together.

7. POSIX requires that implementations of standard I/O (printf, fprintf, fwrite, fread, etc) are thread safe. Unfortunately GNU libc implements this by using internal locking primitives that Helgrind is unable to intercept. Consequently Helgrind generates many false race reports when you use these functions.

   Helgrind attempts to hide these errors using the standard Valgrind error-suppression mechanism. So, at least for simple test cases, you don't see any. Nevertheless, some may slip through. Just something to be aware of.

8. Helgrind's error checks do not work properly inside the system threading library itself (libpthread.so), and it usually observes large numbers of (false) errors in there. Valgrind's suppression system then filters these out, so you should not see them.

   If you see any race errors reported where libpthread.so or ld.so is the object associated with the innermost stack frame, please file a bug report at http://www.valgrind.org.

9.6 Helgrind Options

The following end-user options are available:

- `--happens-before=none|threads|all` [default: all]

  Helgrind always regards locks as the basis for inter-thread synchronisation. However, by default, before reporting a race error, Helgrind will also check whether certain other kinds of inter-thread synchronisation events happened. It may be that if such events took place, then no race really occurred, and so no error needs to be reported. See Section 9.4.3 [Excl Transfers], page 104 for a discussion of transfers of exclusive ownership states between threads.

  With `--happens-before=all`, the following events are regarded as sources of synchronisation: thread creation/joinage, condition variable signal/broadcast/waits, and semaphore posts/waits.

  With `--happens-before=threads`, only thread creation/joinage events are regarded as sources of synchronisation.

  With `--happens-before=none`, no events (apart, of course, from locking) are regarded as sources of synchronisation.

  Changing this setting from the default will increase your false-error rate but give little or no gain. The only advantage is that `--happens-before=threads` and `--happens-before=none` should make Helgrind less and less sensitive to the scheduling of threads, and hence the output more and more repeatable across runs.

- `--trace-addr=0xXXYYZZ` and `--trace-level=0|1|2` [default: 1]

  Requests that Helgrind produces a log of all state changes to location 0xXXYYZZ. This can be helpful in tracking down tricky races. `--trace-level` controls the verbosity of the log. At the default setting (1), a one-line summary of is printed for each state change. At level 2 a complete stack trace is printed for each state change.

In addition, the following debugging options are available for Helgrind:

- `--trace-malloc=no|yes` [no]

  Show all client malloc (etc) and free (etc) requests.

- `--gen-vcg=no|yes|yes-w-vts` [no]

  At exit, write to stderr a dump of the happens-before graph computed by Helgrind, in a format suitable for the VCG graph visualisation tool. A suitable command line is:

  ```
  valgrind --tool=helgrind --gen-vcg=yes my_app 2>&1 | grep xxxxxx
  | sed ''s/xxxxxx//g'' | xvcg -
  ```

  With `--gen-vcg=yes`, the basic happens-before graph is shown. With `--gen-vcg=yes-w-vts`, the vector timestamp for each node is also shown.

- `--cmp-race-err-addrs=no|yes [no]`

  Controls whether or not race (data) addresses should be taken into account when removing duplicates of race errors. With `--cmp-race-err-addrs=no`, two otherwise identical race errors will be considered to be the same if their race addresses differ. With With `--cmp-race-err-addrs=yes` they will be considered different. This is provided to help make certain regression tests work reliably.

- `--hg-sanity-flags=<XXXXXX> (X = 0|1) [000000]`

  Run extensive sanity checks on Helgrind's internal data structures at events defined by the bitstring, as follows:

  100000 at every query to the happens-before graph

  010000 after changes to the lock order acquisition graph

  001000 after every client memory access (NB: not currently used)

  000100 after every client memory range permission setting of 256 bytes or greater

  000010 after every client lock or unlock event

  000001 after every client thread creation or joinage event

  Note these will make Helgrind run very slowly, often to the point of being completely unusable.

9.7 A To-Do List for Helgrind

The following is a list of loose ends which should be tidied up some time.

- Track which mutexes are associated with which condition variables, and emit a warning if this becomes inconsistent.
- For lock order errors, print the complete lock cycle, rather than only doing for size-2 cycles as at present.
- Document the `VALGRIND_HG_CLEAN_MEMORY` client request.
- Possibly a client request to forcibly transfer ownership of memory from one thread to another. Requires further consideration.
- Add a new client request that marks an address range as being "shared-modified with empty lockset" (the error state), and describe how to use it.
- Document races caused by gcc's thread-unsafe code generation for speculative stores.[1]
- Don't update the lock-order graph, and don't check for errors, when a "try"-style lock operation happens (e.g. pthread_mutex_trylock). Such calls do not add any real restrictions to the locking order, since they can always fail to acquire the lock, resulting in the caller going off and doing Plan B (presumably it will have a Plan B). Doing such checks could generate false lock-order errors and confuse users.

---

[1] In the interim see http://gcc.gnu.org/ml/gcc/2007-10/msg00266.html and http://lkml.org/lkml/2007/10/24/673.

- Performance can be very poor. Slowdowns on the order of 100:1 are not unusual. There is quite some scope for performance improvements, though.

10 Nulgrind: the null tool

Nulgrind is the minimal tool for Valgrind. It does no initialisation or finalisation, and adds no instrumentation to the program's code. It is mainly of use for Valgrind's developers for debugging and regression testing.

Nonetheless you can run programs with Nulgrind. They will run roughly 5 times more slowly than normal, for no useful effect. Note that you need to use the option --tool=none to run Nulgrind (i.e. not --tool=nulgrind).

11 Lackey: a simple profiler and memory tracer

To use this tool, you must specify `--tool=lackey` on the Valgrind command line.

11.1 Overview

Lackey is a simple valgrind tool that does some basic program measurement. It adds quite a lot of simple instrumentation to the program's code. It is primarily intended to be of use as an example tool, and consequently emphasises clarity of implementation over performance.

It measures and reports various things.

1. When command line option `--basic-counts=yes` is specified, it prints the following statistics and information about the execution of the client program:

   1. The number of calls to `_dl_runtime_resolve()`, the function in glibc's dynamic linker that resolves function references to shared objects.

      You can change the name of the function tracked with command line option `--fnname=<name>`.

   2. The number of conditional branches encountered and the number and proportion of those taken.

   3. The number of superblocks entered and completed by the program. Note that due to optimisations done by the JIT, this is not at all an accurate value.

   4. The number of guest (x86, amd64, ppc, etc.) instructions and IR statements executed. IR is Valgrind's RISC-like intermediate representation via which all instrumentation is done.

   5. Ratios between some of these counts.

   6. The exit code of the client program.

2. When command line option `--detailed-counts=yes` is specified, a table is printed with counts of loads, stores and ALU operations for various types of operands.

   The types are identified by their IR name (I1 ... I128, F32, F64, and V128).

3. When command line option `--trace-mem=yes` is specified, it prints out the size and address of almost every load and store made by the program. See the comments at the top of the file `lackey/lk_main.c` for details about the output format, how it works, and inaccuracies in the address trace.

4. When command line option --trace-superblocks=yes is specified, it prints out the address of every superblock (extended basic block) executed by the program. This is primarily of interest to Valgrind developers. See the comments at the top of the file lackey/lk_main.c for details about the output format.

Note that Lackey runs quite slowly, especially when the option --detailed-counts=yes is specified. It could be made to run a lot faster by doing a slightly more sophisticated job of the instrumentation, but that would undermine its role as a simple example tool. Hence we have chosen not to do so.

Note also that --trace-mem=yes and --trace-superblocks=yes create immense amounts of output. If you are saving the output in a file, you can eat up tens of gigabytes of disk space very quickly. As a result of printing out so much stuff, they also cause the program to run absolutely utterly unbelievably slowly.

11.2 Lackey Options

Lackey-specific options are:

- --basic-counts=<no|yes> [default: yes]

  Count basic events, as described above.

- --detailed-counts=<no|yes> [default: no]

  Count loads, stores and alu ops, differentiated by their IR types.

- --fnname=<name> [default: _dl_runtime_resolve()]

  Count calls to the function <name>.

- --trace-mem=<no|yes> [default: no]

  Produce a log of all memory references, as described above.

- --trace-superblocks=<no|yes> [default: no]

  Print a line of text giving the address of each superblock (single entry, multiple exit chunk of code) executed by the program.

12 Valgrind FAQ

Background:

- How do you pronounce "Valgrind"?

  Answer: The "Val" as in the world "value". The "grind" is pronounced with a short 'i'—i.e. "grinned" (rhymes with "tinned") rather than "grined" (rhymes with "find").

  Don't feel bad: almost everyone gets it wrong at first.

- Where does the name "Valgrind" come from?

  Answer: From Nordic mythology. Originally (before release) the project was named Heimdall, after the watchman of the Nordic gods. He could "see a hundred miles by day or night, hear the grass growing, see the wool growing on a sheep's back" (etc). This would have been a great name, but it was already taken by a security package "Heimdal".

  Keeping with the Nordic theme, Valgrind was chosen. Valgrind is the name of the main entrance to Valhalla (the Hall of the Chosen Slain in Asgard). Over this entrance there resides a wolf and over it there is the head of a boar and on it perches a huge eagle, whose eyes can see to the far regions of the nine worlds. Only those judged worthy by the guardians are allowed to pass through Valgrind. All others are refused entrance.

  It's not short for "value grinder", although that's not a bad guess.

Compiling, installing and configuring:

- When I try building Valgrind, make dies partway with an assertion failure, something like this:

  ```
  $ make:  expand.c:489: allocated_variable_append:
           Assertion 'current_variable_set_list->next
           != 0' failed.
  ```

  Answer: It's probably a bug in make. Some, but not all, instances of version 3.79.1 have this bug, see www.mail-archive.com/bug-make@gnu.org/msg01658.html. Try upgrading to a more recent version of make. Alternatively, we have heard that unsetting the CFLAGS environment variable avoids the problem.

- When I try to build Valgrind, make fails with

  ```
  /usr/bin/ld: cannot find -lc
  collect2: ld returned 1 exit status
  ```

  Answer: You need to install the glibc-static-devel package.

Valgrind aborts unexpectedly:

- Programs run OK on Valgrind, but at exit produce a bunch of errors involving __libc_freeres() and then die with a segmentation fault.

  Answer: When the program exits, Valgrind runs the procedure __libc_freeres() in glibc. This is a hook for memory debuggers, so they can ask glibc to free up any memory it has used. Doing that is needed to ensure that Valgrind doesn't incorrectly report space leaks in glibc.

  Problem is that running __libc_freeres() in older glibc versions causes this crash.

  Workaround for 1.1.X and later versions of Valgrind: use the --run-libc-freeres=no flag. You may then get space leak reports for glibc allocations (please don't report these to the glibc people, since they are not real leaks), but at least the program runs.

- My (buggy) program dies like this:

        valgrind: m_mallocfree.c:442 (bszW_to_pszW):
          Assertion 'pszW >= 0' failed.

  Answer: If Memcheck (the memory checker) shows any invalid reads, invalid writes or invalid frees in your program, the above may happen. Reason is that your program may trash Valgrind's low-level memory manager, which then dies with the above assertion, or something similar. The cure is to fix your program so that it doesn't do any illegal memory accesses. The above failure will hopefully go away after that.

- My program dies, printing a message like this along the way:

        vex x86->IR: unhandled instruction bytes:
          0x66 0xF 0x2E 0x5

  Answer: Older versions did not support some x86 and amd64 instructions, particularly SSE/SSE2/SSE3 instructions. Try a newer Valgrind; we now support almost all instructions. If it still breaks, file a bug report.

  Another possibility is that your program has a bug and erroneously jumps to a non-code address, in which case you'll get a SIGILL signal. Memcheck may issue a warning just before this happens, but it might not if the jump happens to land in addressable memory.

- I tried running a Java program (or another program that uses a just-in-time compiler) under Valgrind but something went wrong. Does Valgrind handle such programs?

  Answer: Valgrind can handle dynamically generated code, so long as none of the generated code is later overwritten by other generated code. If this happens, though, things will go wrong as Valgrind will continue running its translations of the old code (this is true on x86 and amd64, on PowerPC there are explicit cache flush instructions which Valgrind detects and honours). You should try running with --smc-check=all in this case. Valgrind will run much more slowly, but should detect the use of the out-of-date code.

  Alternatively, if you have the source code to the JIT compiler you can insert calls to the VALGRIND_DISCARD_TRANSLATIONS client request to mark out-of-date code, saving you from using --smc-check=all.

Apart from this, in theory Valgrind can run any Java program just fine, even those that use JNI and are partially implemented in other languages like C and C++. In practice, Java implementations tend to do nasty things that most programs do not, and Valgrind sometimes falls over these corner cases.

If your Java programs do not run under Valgrind, even with `--smc-check=all`, please file a bug report and hopefully we'll be able to fix the problem.

Valgrind behaves unexpectedly:

- My program uses the C++ STL and string classes. Valgrind reports 'still reachable' memory leaks involving these classes at the exit of the program, but there should be none.

  Answer: First of all: relax, it's probably not a bug, but a feature. Many implementations of the C++ standard libraries use their own memory pool allocators. Memory for quite a number of destructed objects is not immediately freed and given back to the OS, but kept in the pool(s) for later re-use. The fact that the pools are not freed at the exit() of the program cause Valgrind to report this memory as still reachable. The behaviour not to free pools at the exit() could be called a bug of the library though.

  Using gcc, you can force the STL to use malloc and to free memory as soon as possible by globally disabling memory caching. Beware! Doing so will probably slow down your program, sometimes drastically.

  - With gcc 2.91, 2.95, 3.0 and 3.1, compile all source using the STL with `-D__USE_MALLOC`. Beware! This was removed from gcc starting with version 3.3.

  - With gcc 3.2.2 and later, you should export the environment variable `GLIBCPP_FORCE_NEW` before running your program.

  - With gcc 3.4 and later, that variable has changed name to `GLIBCXX_FORCE_NEW`.

  There are other ways to disable memory pooling: using the `malloc_alloc` template with your objects (not portable, but should work for gcc) or even writing your own memory allocators. But all this goes beyond the scope of this FAQ. Start by reading the libstdc++ documentation[1] if you absolutely want to do that. But beware: allocators belong to the more messy parts of the STL and people went to great lengths to make the STL portable across platforms. Chances are good that your solution will work on your platform, but not on others.

- The stack traces given by Memcheck (or another tool) aren't helpful. How can I improve them?

  Answer: If they're not long enough, use `--num-callers` to make them longer.

---

[1] http://gcc.gnu.org/onlinedocs/libstdc++/faq/index.html#4_4_leak

If they're not detailed enough, make sure you are compiling with -g to add
debug information. And don't strip symbol tables (programs should be
unstripped unless you run 'strip' on them; some libraries ship stripped).

Also, for leak reports involving shared objects, if the shared object is
unloaded before the program terminates, Valgrind will discard the debug information and the error message will be full of ??? entries. The
workaround here is to avoid calling dlclose() on these shared objects.

Also, -fomit-frame-pointer and -fstack-check can make stack traces
worse.

Some example sub-traces:

- With debug information and unstripped (best):

    ```
    Invalid write of size 1
        at 0x80483BF: really (malloc1.c:20)
        by 0x8048370: main (malloc1.c:9)
    ```

- With no debug information, unstripped:

    ```
    Invalid write of size 1
        at 0x80483BF: really (in a.out)
        by 0x8048370: main (in a.out)
    ```

- With no debug information, stripped:

    ```
    Invalid write of size 1
        at 0x80483BF: (within a.out)
        by 0x8048370: (within a.out)
        by 0x42015703: __libc_start_main
                       (in /lib/tls/libc-2.3.2.so)
        by 0x80482CC: (within a.out)
    ```

- With debug information and -fomit-frame-pointer:

    ```
    Invalid write of size 1
        at 0x80483C4: really (malloc1.c:20)
        by 0x42015703: __libc_start_main
        (in /lib/tls/libc-2.3.2.so)
        by 0x80482CC: ??? (start.S:81)
    ```

- A leak error message involving an unloaded shared object:

    ```
    84 bytes in 1 blocks are possibly lost in
      loss record 488 of 713
        at 0x1B9036DA: operator new(unsigned)
        (vg_replace_malloc.c:132)
        by 0x1DB63EEB: ???
        by 0x1DB4B800: ???
        by 0x1D65E007: ???
        by 0x8049EE6: main (main.cpp:24)
    ```

- The stack traces given by Memcheck (or another tool) seem to have the wrong function name in them. What's happening?

  Answer: Occasionally Valgrind stack traces get the wrong function names. This is caused by glibc using aliases to effectively give one function two names. Most of the time Valgrind chooses a suitable name, but very occasionally it gets it wrong. Examples we know of are printing 'bcmp' instead of 'memcmp', 'index' instead of 'strchr', and 'rindex' instead of 'strrchr'.

- My program crashes normally, but doesn't under Valgrind, or vice versa. What's happening?

  Answer: When a program runs under Valgrind, its environment is slightly different to when it runs natively. For example, the memory layout is different, and the way that threads are scheduled is different.

  Most of the time this doesn't make any difference, but it can, particularly if your program is buggy. For example, if your program crashes because it erroneously accesses memory that is unaddressable, it's possible that this memory will not be unaddressable when run under Valgrind. Alternatively, if your program has data races, these may not manifest under Valgrind.

  There isn't anything you can do to change this, it's just the nature of the way Valgrind works that it cannot exactly replicate a native execution environment. In the case where your program crashes due to a memory error when run natively but not when run under Valgrind, in most cases Memcheck should identify the bad memory operation.

Memcheck doesn't find my bug:

- I try running `valgrind --tool=memcheck my_program` and get Valgrind's startup message, but I don't get any errors and I know my program has errors.

  Answer: There are two possible causes of this.

  First, by default, Valgrind only traces the top-level process. So if your program spawns children, they won't be traced by Valgrind by default. Also, if your program is started by a shell script, Perl script, or something similar, Valgrind will trace the shell, or the Perl interpreter, or equivalent.

  To trace child processes, use the `--trace-children=yes` option.

  If you are tracing large trees of processes, it can be less disruptive to have the output sent over the network. Give Valgrind the flag `--log-socket=127.0.0.1:12345` (if you want logging output sent to port 12345 on localhost). You can use the valgrind-listener program to listen on that port:

  ```
  valgrind-listener 12345
  ```

  Obviously you have to start the listener process first. See the manual for more details.

  Second, if your program is statically linked, most Valgrind tools won't work as well, because they won't be able to replace certain functions, such as malloc(), with their own versions. A key indicator of this is if Memcheck says:

```
All heap blocks were freed -- no leaks are possible
```

when you know your program calls malloc(). The workaround is to avoid statically linking your program.

- Why doesn't Memcheck find the array overruns in this program?

```
int static[5];

int main(void)
{
  int stack[5];

  static[5] = 0;
  stack [5] = 0;

  return 0;
}
```

Answer: Unfortunately, Memcheck doesn't do bounds checking on static or stack arrays. We'd like to, but it's just not possible to do in a reasonable way that fits with how Memcheck works. Sorry.

Miscellaneous:

- I tried writing a suppression but it didn't work. Can you write my suppression for me?

  Answer: Yes! Use the --gen-suppressions=yes feature to spit out suppressions automatically for you. You can then edit them if you like, e.g. combining similar automatically generated suppressions using wildcards like '*'.

  If you really want to write suppressions by hand, read the manual carefully. Note particularly that C++ function names must be mangled (that is, not demangled).

- With Memcheck's memory leak detector, what's the difference between "definitely lost", "possibly lost", "still reachable", and "suppressed"?

  Answer: The details are in the Memcheck section of the user manual.

  In short:

  - "definitely lost" means your program is leaking memory—fix it!
  - "possibly lost" means your program is probably leaking memory, unless you're doing funny things with pointers.
  - "still reachable" means your program is probably ok—it didn't free some memory it could have. This is quite common and often reasonable. Don't use --show-reachable=yes if you don't want to see these reports.
  - "suppressed" means that a leak error has been suppressed. There are some suppressions in the default suppression files. You can ignore suppressed errors.

- Memcheck's uninitialised value errors are hard to track down, because they are often reported some time after they are caused. Could Memcheck record a trail of operations to better link the cause to the effect? Or maybe just eagerly report any copies of uninitialised memory values?

Answer: We'd love to improve these errors, but we don't know how to do it without huge performance penalties.

You can use the client request VALGRIND_CHECK_VALUE_IS_DEFINED to help track these errors down—work backwards from the point where the uninitialised error occurs, checking suspect values until you find the cause. This requires editing, compiling and re-running your program multiple times, which is a pain, but still easier than debugging the problem without Memcheck's help.

As for eager reporting of copies of uninitialised memory values, this has been suggested multiple times. Unfortunately, almost all programs legitimately copy uninitialised memory values around (because compilers pad structs to preserve alignment) and eager checking leads to hundreds of false positives. Therefore Memcheck does not support eager checking at this time.

How To Get Further Assistance:

Answer: Please read all of this section before posting.

If you think an answer is incomplete or inaccurate, please e-mail valgrind@valgrind.org.

Read the appropriate section(s) of the Valgrind Documentation.

Read the Distribution Documents.

Search the valgrind-users mailing list archives, using the group name gmane.comp.debugging.valgrind.

Only when you have tried all of these things and are still stuck, should you post to the valgrind-users mailing list. In which case, please read the following carefully. Making a complete posting will greatly increase the chances that an expert or fellow user reading it will have enough information and motivation to reply.

Make sure you give full details of the problem, including the full output of valgrind -v <your-prog>, if applicable. Also which Linux distribution you're using (Red Hat, Debian, etc) and its version number.

You are in little danger of making your posting too long unless you include large chunks of Valgrind's (unsuppressed) output, so err on the side of giving too much information.

Clearly written subject lines and message bodies are appreciated, too.

Finally, remember that, despite the fact that most of the community are very helpful and responsive to emailed questions, you are probably requesting help from unpaid volunteers, so you have no guarantee of receiving an answer.

13 Callgrind Format Specification

This chapter describes the Callgrind Profile Format, Version 1.

A synonymous name is "Calltree Profile Format". These names actually mean the same since Callgrind was previously named Calltree.

The format description is meant for the user to be able to understand the file contents; but more important, it is given for authors of measurement or visualization tools to be able to write and read this format.

13.1 Overview

The profile data format is ASCII based. It is written by Callgrind, and it is upwards compatible to the format used by Cachegrind (i.e. Cachegrind uses a subset). It can be read by callgrind_annotate and KCachegrind.

This chapter gives on overview of format features and examples. For detailed syntax, look at the format reference.

13.1.1 Basic Structure

Each file has a header part of an arbitrary number of lines of the format "key: value". The lines with key "positions" and "events" define the meaning of cost lines in the second part of the file: the value of "positions" is a list of subpositions, and the value of "events" is a list of event type names. Cost lines consist of subpositions followed by 64-bit counters for the events, in the order specified by the "positions" and "events" header line.

The "events" header line is always required in contrast to the optional line for "positions", which defaults to "line", i.e. a line number of some source file. In addition, the second part of the file contains position specifications of the form "spec=name". "spec" can be e.g. "fn" for a function name or "fl" for a file name. Cost lines are always related to the function/file specifications given directly before.

13.1.2 Simple Example

The event names in the following example are quite arbitrary, and are not related to event names used by Callgrind. Especially, cycle counts matching real processors probably will never be generated by any Valgrind tools, as these are bound to simulations of simple machine models for acceptable slowdown. However, any profiling tool could use the format described in this chapter.

```
events: Cycles Instructions Flops
fl=file.f
fn=main
15 90 14 2
16 20 12
```

The above example gives profile information for event types "Cycles", "Instructions", and "Flops". Thus, cost lines give the number of CPU cycles passed by, number of executed instructions, and number of floating point operations executed while running code corresponding to some source position. As there is no line specifying the value of "positions", it defaults to "line", which means that the first number of a cost line is always a line number.

Thus, the first cost line specifies that in line 15 of source file 'file.f' there is code belonging to function main. While running, 90 CPU cycles passed by, and 2 of the 14 instructions executed were floating point operations. Similarly, the next line specifies that there were 12 instructions executed in the context of function main which can be related to line 16 in file 'file.f', taking 20 CPU cycles. If a cost line specifies less event counts than given in the "events" line, the rest is assumed to be zero. I.e., there was no floating point instruction executed relating to line 16.

Note that regular cost lines always give self (also called exclusive) cost of code at a given position. If you specify multiple cost lines for the same position, these will be summed up. On the other hand, in the example above there is no specification of how many times function main actually was called: profile data only contains sums.

13.1.3 Associations

The most important extension to the original format of Cachegrind is the ability to specify call relationship among functions. More generally, you specify associations among positions. For this, the second part of the file also can contain association specifications. These look similar to position specifications, but consist of 2 lines. For calls, the format looks like

```
calls=(Call Count) (Destination position)
(Source position) (Inclusive cost of call)
```

The destination only specifies subpositions like line number. Therefore, to be able to specify a call to another function in another source file, you have to precede the above lines with a "cfn=" specification for the name of the called function, and a "cfl=" specification if the function is in another source file. The 2nd line looks like a regular cost line with the difference that inclusive cost spent inside of the function call has to be specified.

Other associations which or for example (conditional) jumps. See the reference below for details.

13.1.4 Extended Example

The following example shows 3 functions, main, func1, and func2. Function main calls func1 once and func2 3 times. func1 calls func2 2 times.

```
events: Instructions

fl=file1.c
fn=main
16 20
cfn=func1
calls=1 50
16 400
cfl=file2.c
cfn=func2
calls=3 20
```

```
16 400

fn=func1
51 100
cfl=file2.c
cfn=func2
calls=2 20
51 300

fl=file2.c
fn=func2
20 700
```

One can see that in main only code from line 16 is executed where also the other functions are called. Inclusive cost of main is 820, which is the sum of self cost 20 and costs spent in the calls: 400 for the single call to func1 and 400 as sum for the three calls to func2.

Function func1 is located in 'file1.c', the same as main. Therefore, a cfl= specification for the call to func1 is not needed. The function func1 only consists of code at line 51 of 'file1.c', where func2 is called.

13.1.5 Name Compression

With the introduction of association specifications like calls it is needed to specify the same function or same file name multiple times. As absolute file-names or symbol names in C++ can be quite long, it is advantageous to be able to specify integer IDs for position specifications. Here, the term "position" corresponds to a file name (source or object file) or function name.

To support name compression, a position specification can be not only of the format spec=name, but also spec=(ID) name to specify a mapping of an integer ID to a name, and spec=(ID) to reference a previously defined ID mapping. There is a separate ID mapping for each position specification, i.e. you can use ID 1 for both a file name and a symbol name.

With string compression, the example from 1.4 looks like this:

```
events: Instructions

fl=(1) file1.c
fn=(1) main
16 20
cfn=(2) func1
calls=1 50
16 400
cfl=(2) file2.c
cfn=(3) func2
calls=3 20
16 400

fn=(2)
51 100
```

```
cfl=(2)
cfn=(3)
calls=2 20
51 300

fl=(2)
fn=(3)
20 700
```

As position specifications carry no information themselves, but only change
the meaning of subsequent cost lines or associations, they can appear everywhere
in the file without any negative consequence. Especially, you can define name
compression mappings directly after the header, and before any cost lines. Thus,
the above example can also be written as

```
events: Instructions

# define file ID mapping
fl=(1) file1.c
fl=(2) file2.c
# define function ID mapping
fn=(1) main
fn=(2) func1
fn=(3) func2

fl=(1)
fn=(1)
16 20
...
```

13.1.6 Subposition Compression

If a Callgrind data file should hold costs for each assembler instruction of a
program, you specify subposition "instr" in the "positions:" header line, and
each cost line has to include the address of some instruction. Addresses are
allowed to have a size of 64bit to support 64bit architectures. Thus, repeating
similar, long addresses for almost every line in the data file can enlarge the file
size quite significantly, and motivates for subposition compression: instead of
every cost line starting with a 16 character long address, one is allowed to specify
relative addresses. This relative specification is not only allowed for instruction
addresses, but also for line numbers; both addresses and line numbers are called
"subpositions".

A relative subposition always is based on the corresponding subposition of the
last cost line, and starts with a + to specify a positive difference, a - to specify
a negative difference, or consists of * to specify the same subposition. Because
absolute subpositions always are positive (i.e. never prefixed by -), any relative
specification is non-ambiguous; additionally, absolute and relative subposition
specifications can be mixed freely. Assume the following example (subpositions
can always be specified as hexadecimal numbers, beginning with 0x):

```
positions: instr line
events: ticks

fn=func
0x80001234 90 1
0x80001237 90 5
0x80001238 91 6
```

With subposition compression, this looks like

```
positions: instr line
events: ticks

fn=func
0x80001234 90 1
+3 * 5
+1 +1 6
```

Remark: For assembler annotation to work, instruction addresses have to be corrected to correspond to addresses found in the original binary. I.e. for relocatable shared objects, often a load offset has to be subtracted.

13.1.7 Miscellaneous

13.1.7.1 Cost Summary Information

For the visualization to be able to show cost percentage, a sum of the cost of the full run has to be known. Usually, it is assumed that this is the sum of all cost lines in a file. But sometimes, this is not correct. Thus, you can specify a "summary:" line in the header giving the full cost for the profile run. This has another effect: a import filter can show a progress bar while loading a large data file if he knows to cost sum in advance.

13.1.7.2 Long Names for Event Types and inherited Types

Event types for cost lines are specified in the "events:" line with an abbreviated name. For visualization, it makes sense to be able to specify some longer, more descriptive name. For an event type "Ir" which means "Instruction Fetches", this can be specified the header line

```
event: Ir : Instruction Fetches
events: Ir Dr
```

In this example, "Dr" itself has no long name associated. The order of "event:" lines and the "events:" line is of no importance. Additionally, inherited event types can be introduced for which no raw data is available, but which are calculated from given types. Suppose the last example, you could add

```
event: Sum = Ir + Dr
```

to specify an additional event type "Sum", which is calculated by adding costs for "Ir" and "Dr".

13.2 Reference

13.2.1 Grammar

```
ProfileDataFile := FormatVersion? Creator? PartData*
FormatVersion := "version:" Space* Number "\n"
Creator := "creator:" NoNewLineChar* "\n"
PartData := (HeaderLine "\n")+ (BodyLine "\n")+
HeaderLine := (empty line)
  | ('#' NoNewLineChar*)
  | PartDetail
  | Description
  | EventSpecification
  | CostLineDef
PartDetail := TargetCommand | TargetID
TargetCommand := "cmd:" Space* NoNewLineChar*
TargetID := ("pid"|"thread"|"part") ":" Space* Number
Description := "desc:" Space* Name Space* ":" NoNewLineChar*
EventSpecification := "event:" Space* Name InheritedDef?
  LongNameDef?
InheritedDef := "=" InheritedExpr
InheritedExpr := Name
  | Number Space* ("*" Space*)? Name
  | InheritedExpr Space* "+" Space* InheritedExpr
LongNameDef := ":" NoNewLineChar*
CostLineDef := "events:" Space* Name (Space+ Name)*
  | "positions:" "instr"? (Space+ "line")?
BodyLine := (empty line)
  | ('#' NoNewLineChar*)
  | CostLine
  | PositionSpecification
  | AssociationSpecification
CostLine := SubPositionList Costs?
SubPositionList := (SubPosition+ Space+)+
SubPosition := Number | "+" Number | "-" Number | "*"
Costs := (Number Space+)+
PositionSpecification := Position "=" Space* PositionName
Position := CostPosition | CalledPosition
CostPosition := "ob" | "fl" | "fi" | "fe" | "fn"
CalledPosition := " "cob" | "cfl" | "cfn"
PositionName := ( "(" Number ")" )? (Space* NoNewLineChar* )?
AssociationSpecification := CallSpecification
  | JumpSpecification
CallSpecification := CallLine "\n" CostLine
```

```
CallLine := "calls=" Space* Number Space+ SubPositionList
JumpSpecification := ...
Space := " " | "\t"
Number := HexNumber | (Digit)+
Digit := "0" | ... | "9"
HexNumber := "0x" (Digit | HexChar)+
HexChar := "a" | ... | "f" | "A" | ... | "F"
Name = Alpha (Digit | Alpha)*
Alpha = "a" | ... | "z" | "A" | ... | "Z"
NoNewLineChar := all characters without "\n"
```

13.2.2 Description of Header Lines

The header has an arbitrary number of lines of the format "key: value". Possible *key* values for the header are:

- version: number [Callgrind]

  This is used to distinguish future profile data formats. A major version of 0 or 1 is supposed to be upwards compatible with Cachegrind's format. It is optional; if not appearing, version 1 is supposed. Otherwise, this has to be the first header line.

- pid: process id [Callgrind]

  This specifies the process ID of the supervised application for which this profile was generated.

- cmd: program name + args [Cachegrind]

  This specifies the full command line of the supervised application for which this profile was generated.

- part: number [Callgrind]

  This specifies a sequentially incremented number for each dump generated, starting at 1.

- desc: type: value [Cachegrind]

  This specifies various information for this dump. For some types, the semantic is defined, but any description type is allowed. Unknown types should be ignored.

  There are the types "I1 cache", "D1 cache", "L2 cache", which specify parameters used for the cache simulator. These are the only types originally used by Cachegrind. Additionally, Callgrind uses the following types: "Timerange" gives a rough range of the basic block counter, for which the cost of this dump was collected. Type "Trigger" states the reason of why this trace was generated. E.g. program termination or forced interactive dump.

- `positions: [instr] [line]` [Callgrind]

  For cost lines, this defines the semantic of the first numbers. Any combination of "instr", "bb" and "line" is allowed, but has to be in this order which corresponds to position numbers at the start of the cost lines later in the file.

  If "instr" is specified, the position is the address of an instruction whose execution raised the events given later on the line. This address is relative to the offset of the binary/shared library file to not have to specify relocation info. For "line", the position is the line number of a source file, which is responsible for the events raised. Note that the mapping of "instr" and "line" positions are given by the debugging line information produced by the compiler.

  This field is optional. If not specified, "line" is supposed only.

- `events: event type abbreviations` [Cachegrind]

  A list of short names of the event types logged in this file. The order is the same as in cost lines. The first event type is the second or third number in a cost line, depending on the value of "positions". Callgrind does not add additional cost types. Specify exactly once.

  Cost types from original Cachegrind are:

  - `Ir`: Instruction read access
  - `I1mr`: Instruction Level 1 read cache miss
  - `I2mr`: Instruction Level 2 read cache miss
  - ...

- `summary: costs` [Callgrind]

  `totals: costs` [Cachegrind]

  The value or the total number of events covered by this trace file. Both keys have the same meaning, but the "totals:" line happens to be at the end of the file, while "summary:" appears in the header. This was added to allow postprocessing tools to know in advance to total cost. The two lines always give the same cost counts.

13.2.3 Description of Body Lines

There exist lines `spec=position`. The values for position specifications are arbitrary strings. When starting with (and a digit, it's a string in compressed format. Otherwise it's the real position string. This allows for file and symbol names as position strings, as these never start with (+ *digit*. The compressed format is either (*number*) *space position* or only (*number*). The first relates *position* to *number* in the context of the given format specification from this line to the end of the file; it makes the (*number*) an alias for *position*. Compressed format is always optional.

Position specifications allowed:

- `ob=` [Callgrind]

  The ELF object where the cost of next cost lines happens.

- `fl=` [Cachegrind]

- `fi=` [Cachegrind]
- `fe=` [Cachegrind]

  The source file including the code which is responsible for the cost of next cost lines. `fi=`/`fe=` is used when the source file changes inside of a function, i.e. for inlined code.

- `fn=` [Cachegrind]

  The name of the function where the cost of next cost lines happens.

- `cob=` [Callgrind]

  The ELF object of the target of the next call cost lines.

- `cfl=` [Callgrind]

  The source file including the code of the target of the next call cost lines.

- `cfn=` [Callgrind]

  The name of the target function of the next call cost lines.

- `calls=` [Callgrind]

  The number of nonrecursive calls which are responsible for the cost specified by the next call cost line. This is the cost spent inside of the called function.

  After "calls=" there MUST be a cost line. This is the cost spent in the called function. The first number is the source line from where the call happened.

- `jump=count target position` [Callgrind]

  Unconditional jump, executed count times, to the given target position.

- `jcnd=exe.count jumpcount target position` [Callgrind]

  Conditional jump, executed exe.count times with jumpcount jumps to the given target position.

14 The Design and Implementation of Valgrind

A number of academic publications nicely describe many aspects of Valgrind's design and implementation. Online copies of all of them, and others, are available at http://valgrind.org/docs/pubs.html.

A good top-level overview of Valgrind is given in:

Valgrind: A Framework for Heavyweight Dynamic Binary Instrumentation. Nicholas Nethercote and Julian Seward. Proceedings of ACM SIGPLAN 2007 Conference on Programming Language Design and Implementation (PLDI 2007), San Diego, California, USA, June 2007. This paper describes how Valgrind works, and how it differs from other DBI frameworks such as Pin and DynamoRIO.

The following two papers together give a comprehensive description of how Memcheck works:

Using Valgrind to detect undefined value errors with bit-precision. Julian Seward and Nicholas Nethercote. Proceedings of the USENIX'05 Annual Technical Conference, Anaheim, California, USA, April 2005. This paper describes in detail how Memcheck's undefined value error detection (a.k.a. V bits) works.

How to Shadow Every Byte of Memory Used by a Program. Nicholas Nethercote and Julian Seward. Proceedings of the Third International ACM SIGPLAN/SIGOPS Conference on Virtual Execution Environments (VEE 2007), San Diego, California, USA, June 2007. This paper describes in detail how Memcheck's shadow memory is implemented, and compares it to other alternative approaches.

The following paper describes Callgrind:

A Tool Suite for Simulation Based Analysis of Memory Access Behavior. Josef Weidendorfer, Markus Kowarschik and Carsten Trinitis. Proceedings of the 4th International Conference on Computational Science (ICCS 2004), Krakow, Poland, June 2004. This paper describes Callgrind.

The following dissertation describes Valgrind in some detail (some of these details are now out-of-date) as well as Cachegrind, Annelid and Redux. It also covers some underlying theory about dynamic binary analysis in general and what all these tools have in common:

Dynamic Binary Analysis and Instrumentation. Nicholas Nethercote. PhD Dissertation, University of Cambridge, November 2004.

GNU Free Documentation License

Version 1.2, November 2002
Copyright © 2000,2001,2002 Free Software Foundation, Inc.
51 Franklin St, Fifth Floor, Boston, MA 02110-1301, USA

0. PREAMBLE

The purpose of this License is to make a manual, textbook, or other functional and useful document *free* in the sense of freedom: to assure everyone the effective freedom to copy and redistribute it, with or without modifying it, either commercially or non-commercially. Secondarily, this License preserves for the author and publisher a way to get credit for their work, while not being considered responsible for modifications made by others.

This License is a kind of "copyleft", which means that derivative works of the document must themselves be free in the same sense. It complements the GNU General Public License, which is a copyleft license designed for free software.

We have designed this License in order to use it for manuals for free software, because free software needs free documentation: a free program should come with manuals providing the same freedoms that the software does. But this License is not limited to software manuals; it can be used for any textual work, regardless of subject matter or whether it is published as a printed book. We recommend this License principally for works whose purpose is instruction or reference.

1. APPLICABILITY AND DEFINITIONS

This License applies to any manual or other work, in any medium, that contains a notice placed by the copyright holder saying it can be distributed under the terms of this License. Such a notice grants a world-wide, royalty-free license, unlimited in duration, to use that work under the conditions stated herein. The "Document", below, refers to any such manual or work. Any member of the public is a licensee, and is addressed as "you". You accept the license if you copy, modify or distribute the work in a way requiring permission under copyright law.

A "Modified Version" of the Document means any work containing the Document or a portion of it, either copied verbatim, or with modifications and/or translated into another language.

A "Secondary Section" is a named appendix or a front-matter section of the Document that deals exclusively with the relationship of the publishers or authors of the Document to the Document's overall subject (or to related matters) and contains nothing that could fall directly within that overall subject. (Thus, if the Document is in part a textbook of mathematics, a Secondary Section may not explain any mathematics.) The relationship could be a matter of historical connection with the subject or with related matters, or of legal, commercial, philosophical, ethical or political position regarding them.

The "Invariant Sections" are certain Secondary Sections whose titles are designated, as being those of Invariant Sections, in the notice that says that the Document is released under this License. If a section does not fit the above definition of Secondary then it is not allowed to be designated as Invariant. The Document may contain zero Invariant Sections. If the Document does not identify any Invariant Sections then there are none.

The "Cover Texts" are certain short passages of text that are listed, as Front-Cover Texts or Back-Cover Texts, in the notice that says that the Document is released under this License. A Front-Cover Text may be at most 5 words, and a Back-Cover Text may be at most 25 words.

A "Transparent" copy of the Document means a machine-readable copy, represented in a format whose specification is available to the general public, that is suitable for revising the document straightforwardly with generic text editors or (for images composed of pixels) generic paint programs or (for drawings) some widely available drawing editor, and that is suitable for input to text formatters or for automatic translation to a variety of formats suitable for input to text formatters. A copy made in an otherwise Transparent file format whose markup, or absence of markup, has been arranged to thwart or discourage subsequent modification by readers is not Transparent. An image format is not Transparent if used for any substantial amount of text. A copy that is not "Transparent" is called "Opaque".

Examples of suitable formats for Transparent copies include plain ASCII without markup, Texinfo input format, LaTeX input format, SGML or XML using a publicly available DTD, and standard-conforming simple HTML, PostScript or PDF designed for human modification. Examples of transparent image formats include PNG, XCF and JPG. Opaque formats include proprietary formats that can be read and edited only by proprietary word processors, SGML or XML for which the DTD and/or processing tools are not generally available, and the machine-generated HTML, PostScript or PDF produced by some word processors for output purposes only.

The "Title Page" means, for a printed book, the title page itself, plus such following pages as are needed to hold, legibly, the material this License requires to appear in the title page. For works in formats which do not have any title page as such, "Title Page" means the text near the most prominent appearance of the work's title, preceding the beginning of the body of the text.

A section "Entitled XYZ" means a named subunit of the Document whose title either is precisely XYZ or contains XYZ in parentheses following text that translates XYZ in another language. (Here XYZ stands for a specific section name mentioned below, such as "Acknowledgements", "Dedications", "Endorsements", or "History".) To "Preserve the Title" of such a section when you modify the Document means that it remains a section "Entitled XYZ" according to this definition.

The Document may include Warranty Disclaimers next to the notice which states that this License applies to the Document. These Warranty Disclaimers are considered to be included by reference in this License, but only as regards disclaiming warranties: any other implication that these Warranty Disclaimers may have is void and has no effect on the meaning of this License.

2. VERBATIM COPYING

You may copy and distribute the Document in any medium, either commercially or noncommercially, provided that this License, the copyright notices, and the license notice saying this License applies to the Document are reproduced in all copies, and that you add no other conditions whatsoever to those of this License. You may not use technical measures to obstruct or control the reading or further copying of the copies you make or distribute. However, you may accept compensation in exchange for copies. If you distribute a large enough number of copies you must also follow the conditions in section 3.

You may also lend copies, under the same conditions stated above, and you may publicly display copies.

3. COPYING IN QUANTITY

If you publish printed copies (or copies in media that commonly have printed covers) of the Document, numbering more than 100, and the Document's license notice requires Cover Texts, you must enclose the copies in covers that carry, clearly and legibly, all these Cover Texts: Front-Cover Texts on the front cover, and Back-Cover Texts on the back cover. Both covers must also clearly and legibly identify you as the publisher of these copies. The front cover must present the full title with all words of the title equally prominent and visible. You may add other material on the covers in addition. Copying with changes limited to the covers, as long as they preserve the title of the Document and satisfy these conditions, can be treated as verbatim copying in other respects.

If the required texts for either cover are too voluminous to fit legibly, you should put the first ones listed (as many as fit reasonably) on the actual cover, and continue the rest onto adjacent pages.

If you publish or distribute Opaque copies of the Document numbering more than 100, you must either include a machine-readable Transparent copy along with each Opaque copy, or state in or with each Opaque copy a computer-network location from which the general network-using public has access to download using public-standard network protocols a complete Transparent copy of the Document, free of added material. If you use the latter option, you must take reasonably prudent steps, when you begin distribution of Opaque copies in quantity, to ensure that this Transparent copy will remain thus accessible at the stated location until at least one year after the last time you distribute an Opaque copy (directly or through your agents or retailers) of that edition to the public.

It is requested, but not required, that you contact the authors of the Document well before redistributing any large number of copies, to give them a chance to provide you with an updated version of the Document.

4. MODIFICATIONS

You may copy and distribute a Modified Version of the Document under the conditions of sections 2 and 3 above, provided that you release the Modified Version under precisely this License, with the Modified Version filling the role of the Document, thus licensing distribution and modification of the Modified Version to whoever possesses a copy of it. In addition, you must do these things in the Modified Version:

A. Use in the Title Page (and on the covers, if any) a title distinct from that of the Document, and from those of previous versions (which should, if there were any, be listed in the History section of the Document). You may use the same title as a previous version if the original publisher of that version gives permission.

B. List on the Title Page, as authors, one or more persons or entities responsible for authorship of the modifications in the Modified Version, together with at least five of the principal authors of the Document (all of its principal authors, if it has fewer than five), unless they release you from this requirement.

C. State on the Title page the name of the publisher of the Modified Version, as the publisher.

D. Preserve all the copyright notices of the Document.

E. Add an appropriate copyright notice for your modifications adjacent to the other copyright notices.

F. Include, immediately after the copyright notices, a license notice giving the public permission to use the Modified Version under the terms of this License, in the form shown in the Addendum below.

G. Preserve in that license notice the full lists of Invariant Sections and required Cover Texts given in the Document's license notice.

H. Include an unaltered copy of this License.

I. Preserve the section Entitled "History", Preserve its Title, and add to it an item stating at least the title, year, new authors, and publisher of the Modified Version as given on the Title Page. If there is no section Entitled "History" in the Document, create one stating the title, year, authors, and publisher of the Document as given on its Title Page, then add an item describing the Modified Version as stated in the previous sentence.

J. Preserve the network location, if any, given in the Document for public access to a Transparent copy of the Document, and likewise the network locations given in the Document for previous versions it was based on. These may be placed in the "History" section. You may omit a network location for a work that was published at least four years before the Document itself, or if the original publisher of the version it refers to gives permission.

K. For any section Entitled "Acknowledgements" or "Dedications", Preserve the Title of the section, and preserve in the section all the substance and tone of each of the contributor acknowledgements and/or dedications given therein.

L. Preserve all the Invariant Sections of the Document, unaltered in their text and in their titles. Section numbers or the equivalent are not considered part of the section titles.

M. Delete any section Entitled "Endorsements". Such a section may not be included in the Modified Version.

N. Do not retitle any existing section to be Entitled "Endorsements" or to conflict in title with any Invariant Section.

O. Preserve any Warranty Disclaimers.

If the Modified Version includes new front-matter sections or appendices that qualify as Secondary Sections and contain no material copied from the Document, you may at your option designate some or all of these sections as invariant. To do this, add their titles to the list of Invariant Sections in the Modified Version's license notice. These titles must be distinct from any other section titles.

You may add a section Entitled "Endorsements", provided it contains nothing but endorsements of your Modified Version by various parties—for example, statements of peer review or that the text has been approved by an organization as the authoritative definition of a standard.

You may add a passage of up to five words as a Front-Cover Text, and a passage of up to 25 words as a Back-Cover Text, to the end of the list of Cover Texts in the Modified Version. Only one passage of Front-Cover Text and one of Back-Cover Text may be added by (or through arrangements made by) any one entity. If the Document already includes a cover text for the same cover, previously added by you or by arrangement made by the same entity you are acting on behalf of, you may not add another; but you may replace the old one, on explicit permission from the previous publisher that added the old one.

The author(s) and publisher(s) of the Document do not by this License give permission to use their names for publicity for or to assert or imply endorsement of any Modified Version.

5. COMBINING DOCUMENTS

You may combine the Document with other documents released under this License, under the terms defined in section 4 above for modified versions, provided that you include in the combination all of the Invariant Sections of all of the original documents, unmodified, and list them all as Invariant Sections of your combined work in its license notice, and that you preserve all their Warranty Disclaimers.

The combined work need only contain one copy of this License, and multiple identical Invariant Sections may be replaced with a single copy. If there are multiple Invariant Sections with the same name but different contents, make the title of each such section unique by adding at the end of it, in parentheses, the name of the original author or publisher of that section if known, or else a unique number. Make the same adjustment to the section titles in the list of Invariant Sections in the license notice of the combined work.

In the combination, you must combine any sections Entitled "History" in the various original documents, forming one section Entitled "History"; likewise combine any sections Entitled "Acknowledgements", and any sections Entitled "Dedications". You must delete all sections Entitled "Endorsements."

6. COLLECTIONS OF DOCUMENTS

You may make a collection consisting of the Document and other documents released under this License, and replace the individual copies of this License in the various documents with a single copy that is included in the collection, provided that you follow the rules of this License for verbatim copying of each of the documents in all other respects.

You may extract a single document from such a collection, and distribute it individually under this License, provided you insert a copy of this License into the extracted document, and follow this License in all other respects regarding verbatim copying of that document.

7. AGGREGATION WITH INDEPENDENT WORKS

A compilation of the Document or its derivatives with other separate and independent documents or works, in or on a volume of a storage or distribution medium, is called an "aggregate" if the copyright resulting from the compilation is not used to limit the legal rights of the compilation's users beyond what the individual works permit. When the Document is included in an aggregate, this License does not apply to the other works in the aggregate which are not themselves derivative works of the Document.

If the Cover Text requirement of section 3 is applicable to these copies of the Document, then if the Document is less than one half of the entire aggregate, the Document's Cover Texts may be placed on covers that bracket the Document within the aggregate, or the electronic equivalent of covers if the Document is in electronic form. Otherwise they must appear on printed covers that bracket the whole aggregate.

8. TRANSLATION

Translation is considered a kind of modification, so you may distribute translations of the Document under the terms of section 4. Replacing Invariant Sections with translations requires special permission from their copyright holders, but you may include translations of some or all Invariant Sections in addition to the original versions of these Invariant Sections. You may include a translation of this License, and all the license notices in the Document, and any Warranty Disclaimers, provided that you also include the original English version of this License and the original versions of those notices and disclaimers. In case of a disagreement between the translation and the original version of this License or a notice or disclaimer, the original version will prevail.

If a section in the Document is Entitled "Acknowledgements", "Dedications", or "History", the requirement (section 4) to Preserve its Title (section 1) will typically require changing the actual title.

9. TERMINATION

You may not copy, modify, sublicense, or distribute the Document except as expressly provided for under this License. Any other attempt to copy, modify, sublicense or distribute the Document is void, and will automatically terminate your rights under this License. However, parties who have received copies, or rights, from you under this License will not have their licenses terminated so long as such parties remain in full compliance.

10. FUTURE REVISIONS OF THIS LICENSE

The Free Software Foundation may publish new, revised versions of the GNU Free Documentation License from time to time. Such new versions will be similar in spirit to the present version, but may differ in detail to address new problems or concerns. See http://www.gnu.org/copyleft/.

Each version of the License is given a distinguishing version number. If the Document specifies that a particular numbered version of this License "or any later version" applies to it, you have the option of following the terms and conditions either of that specified version or of any later version that has been published (not as a draft) by the Free Software Foundation. If the Document does not specify a version number of this License, you may choose any version ever published (not as a draft) by the Free Software Foundation.

ADDENDUM: How to use this License for your documents

To use this License in a document you have written, include a copy of the License in the document and put the following copyright and license notices just after the title page:

    Copyright (C) year your name.
    Permission is granted to copy, distribute and/or modify this document
    under the terms of the GNU Free Documentation License, Version 1.2 or
    any later version published by the Free Software Foundation; with no
    Invariant Sections, no Front-Cover Texts, and no Back-Cover Texts. A
    copy of the license is included in the section entitled ''GNU Free
    Documentation License''.

If you have Invariant Sections, Front-Cover Texts and Back-Cover Texts, replace the "with...Texts." line with this:

    with the Invariant Sections being list their titles, with the Front-Cover
    Texts being list, and with the Back-Cover Texts being list.

If you have Invariant Sections without Cover Texts, or some other combination of the three, merge those two alternatives to suit the situation.

If your document contains nontrivial examples of program code, we recommend releasing these examples in parallel under your choice of free software license, such as the GNU General Public License, to permit their use in free software.

History

This section gives the history of the modifications made to the manual by the publisher, as required by the GNU Free Documentation License.

12/2007 "Valgrind User Manual" (original edition)
Source code release 3.3.0 from valgrind.org
Publisher: Valgrind Developers

03/2008 "Valgrind 3.3: Advanced Debugging and Profiling for GNU/Linux applications"
Edited for publication by Brian Gough
Publisher: Network Theory Ltd.
Published under different title, as given above. Added publisher's preface. Minor corrections and modifications for publication as a printed book: reformatted examples to fit smaller page width, removed some long urls to improve line-breaking. Added this "History" section.

The source code for the original version of this document is available from http://valgrind.org/downloads/ in the file 'valgrind-3.3.0.tar.bz2' and for this modified version from http://www.network-theory.co.uk/valgrind/manual/src/.

Books from the publisher

Network Theory publishes books about free software under free documentation licenses. Our current catalogue includes the following titles:

- **PostgreSQL Reference Manual: Volume 1** (ISBN 0-9546120-2-7) $49.95 (£32.00)

  This manual documents the SQL language and commands of PostgreSQL. For each copy of this manual sold, $1 is donated to the PostgreSQL project.

- **PostgreSQL Reference Manual: Volume 2** (ISBN 0-9546120-3-5) $34.95 (£19.95)

  This manual documents the client and server programming interfaces of PostgreSQL. For each copy of this manual sold, $1 is donated to the PostgreSQL project.

- **PostgreSQL Reference Manual: Volume 3** (ISBN 0-9546120-4-3) $24.95 (£13.95)

  This manual is a guide to the configuration and maintenance of PostgreSQL database servers. For each copy of this manual sold, $1 is donated to the PostgreSQL project.

- **GNU Bash Reference Manual** by Chet Ramey and Brian Fox (ISBN 0-9541617-7-7) $29.95 (£19.95)

  This manual is the definitive reference for GNU Bash, the standard GNU command-line interpreter. GNU Bash is a complete implementation of the POSIX.2 Bourne shell specification, with additional features from the C-shell and Korn shell. For each copy of this manual sold, $1 is donated to the Free Software Foundation.

- **Version Management with CVS** by Per Cederqvist et al. (ISBN 0-9541617-1-8) $29.95 (£19.95)

  This manual describes how to use CVS, the concurrent versioning system—one of the most widely-used source-code management systems available today. The manual provides tutorial examples for new users of CVS, as well as the definitive reference documentation for every CVS command and configuration option.

- **Comparing and Merging Files with GNU diff and patch** by David MacKenzie, Paul Eggert, and Richard Stallman (ISBN 0-9541617-5-0) $19.95 (£12.95)

  This manual describes how to compare and merge files using GNU diff and patch. It includes an extensive tutorial that guides the reader through all the options of the diff and patch commands. For each copy of this manual sold, $1 is donated to the Free Software Foundation.

- **An Introduction to GCC** by Brian J. Gough, foreword by Richard M. Stallman. (ISBN 0-9541617-9-3) $19.95 (£12.95)

  This manual provides a tutorial introduction to the GNU C and C++ compilers, gcc and g++. Many books teach the C and C++ languages, but this book explains how to use the compiler itself. Based on years of observation of questions posted on mailing lists, it guides the reader straight to the important options of GCC.

- **An Introduction to Python** by Guido van Rossum and Fred L. Drake, Jr. (ISBN 0-9541617-6-9) $19.95 (£12.95)

  This tutorial provides an introduction to Python, an easy to learn object oriented programming language. For each copy of this manual sold, $1 is donated to the Python Software Foundation.

- **Python Language Reference Manual** by Guido van Rossum and Fred L. Drake, Jr. (ISBN 0-9541617-8-5) $19.95 (£12.95)

  This manual is the official reference for the Python language itself. It describes the syntax of Python and its built-in datatypes in depth, This manual is suitable for readers who need to be familiar with the details and rules of the Python language and its object system. For each copy of this manual sold, $1 is donated to the Python Software Foundation.

- **GNU Octave Manual** by John W. Eaton (ISBN 0-9541617-2-6) $29.99 (£19.99)

  This manual is the definitive guide to GNU Octave, an interactive environment for numerical computation with matrices and vectors. For each copy sold $1 is donated to the GNU Octave Development Fund.

- **GNU Scientific Library Reference Manual—Revised Second Edition** by M. Galassi, et al (ISBN 0-9541617-3-4) $39.99 (£24.99)

  This reference manual is the definitive guide to the GNU Scientific Library (GSL), a numerical library for C and C++ programmers. The manual documents over 1,000 mathematical routines needed for solving problems in science and engineering. All the money raised from the sale of this book supports the development of the GNU Scientific Library.

All titles are available for order from bookstores worldwide.

Sales of the manuals fund the development of more free software and documentation.

For details, visit the website http://www.network-theory.co.uk/

Index

LaVergne, TN USA
24 February 2011

217855LV00002B/176/P